MAKING HEALTH CERTAIN

A Philosophical and Inspirational Treatise
on the Establishment and Maintenance
of Health through a Constructive
Mental Attitude.

BY R. SWINBURNE CLYMER, M. D.
Graduate College of Medicine and
Surgery, Chicago, 1902.

Author of "Diet, The Way to Health",
"Higher Race Development", "The
Way to Happiness", "Race Re-
generation", etc., etc.

♂

Published by
The Humanitarian Society
"Beverly Hall,"
Quakertown, Pa.

Publisher's Note

This edition of "Making Health Certain" is issued as the official publication of the Summer meeting of the Society held at Headquarters, "Beverly Hall," in four sections: First section—July third and ending the fourteenth; second section—July fifteenth and ending the nineteenth; third section—July twentieth and ending the thirtieth; fourth section—August fifth and ending the twelfth, 1921.

The Vision

I lived in an age of strife; all about me were men consumed by ill-will, malice, and hatred. They fought one against the other: class against class; even the children taking part, having knowledge of only the inharmonious life; being ill-shapen and miserable, weakly and sickly, with no light shining from their dullen eyes.

The women were in the background, natural prey to the passions of men; for men had no love for each other; and even in the midst of clans there was mutual distrust of one for the other; while they fought their supposed enemies, not because they loved each other better, but because they hated them more.

Out of the midst of the confusion came a Voice as from heaven and bade me look. As in a cloud of fire there appeared unto me a vision of two divinely perfect beings; their bodies were glorious; as of shining ivory which had life. Out of their eyes looked a Soul of Love; Male and Female were they.

As I gazed inthralled, at their feet appeared children; perfect as the twain. Gradually appeared other full-grown men and women round about them; and in their midst other children; all of them perfect. There was no indication of disease, misery, hatred or discontent; all was harmony; strife and malice had been replaced with love and happiness. As I continued to look upon the glorious vision, a Voice spake unto me:

"This is the new heaven and the new earth, the two become one, and I, thy God, shall be with thee and thy people."
January 8, 1914.

Introductory

The Philosophy-Science-Religion outlined in the present work is admittedly founded on Manhood, a manhood strong, virile, and true; one which, strange as it may at first appear, is in entire harmony with the true conception of Godhood.

During the past centuries mankind has been almost universally taught that to be able to enter the kingdom of heaven, it was necessary for him to deny the body; crucify the flesh; in fact, practically destroy the physical; believing by so doing, he would earn the heavenly reward, a place in the Elysian fields of the Great Hereafter.

Such an abnormal existence was believed to be the means of exalting the soul, though less than one believer out of a thousand ever gave thought to what the soul actually might be, or on what it was dependent for its existence. This was placing a premium on weakness of body; because any doctrine, science, religion, or philosophy that regards the physical vehicle as a hindrance, burden, or a snare to man, is certain to be inducive to neglect of physical welfare.

The new age is at hand, a new cycle has commenced, men are no longer satisfied with the inculcation of a doctrine having in view the debasement of the body that, if possible, the soul might be exalted and God glorified. To be weak, delicate in health, racked with pain, and a victim of disease, will soon be considered a shame rather than an indication of superior godliness; the new Commandment inculcates the truths that man glorifies God by freeing the body of disease and suffering, making it strong, and as nearly perfect as possible. Only through development of body and Soul does man, in very truth, glorify God.

Naturally, the thinker realizes that instructions of this nature, through exaltation of the physical, have a tendency toward prolonging life on earth, leading to immortality. He comprehends that the development of the body, freedom from weakness and disease, and a general physical reconstruction will offer a fuller life and greater opportunity. The question then arises, if it is possible to accomplish all this, is it really desirable, considering the conditions under which man lives at the present time?

Were the answer given without due consideration, it would no doubt be in the negative; because under a regime where sin, sickness, suffering, sorrow, crime, and vice prevail, even three score and ten years are sufficiently long. However, we must not forget that as the new age advances and multitudes commence to comprehend the Greater Philosophy, undesirable conditions will gradually give way to a more enlightened era.

This is not a modern dream, but was clearly foretold ages ago. The ideal state, resulting when men finally attain Conscious Immortality while on earth, was the theme of the writer of Revelations, as witness:

"And I saw a new heaven and a new earth; for the first heaven and the first earth were passed away; and there was no more sea.

"And I, John saw the holy (whole) city, New Jerusalem (the Soul having attained Sonship with God), coming down out of heaven, prepared as a bride adorned for her husband.

"And I heard a great voice out of heaven crying, Behold, the tabernacle of God is with men, and he will dwell with them, and they shall be his people, and God himself shall be with them, and be their God."
—Rev. 21:1-3.

How few of the countless multitudes who have read this Scriptural passage have had even an inkling of its real significance? These words of the inspired writer mean exactly what they say; yet few have thought it possible there might be a great change in both heaven and earth? As a fact, practically no thought has been given to these great truths, and men generally have taken for granted that heaven, which is to say, the place where souls (the immortal part of man) are supposed to have gone after death, should continue to exist throughout the eternal ages. Despite this belief, John, greatest of the Revelators, clearly states that he saw "the first heaven passed away."

Heaven, as generally understood, is the plane of existence where pass to, and remain, the souls of the Departed, existing forever in unalloyed joy. Philosophy terms this plane the Soul World; a sphere of waiting to which souls proceed after the death of the body, and where they remain temporarily, until such time as they may be enabled to return to earth to continue their pilgrimage toward knowledge and development.

To use a homely, but practical, comparison, the Soul World, heaven so-called, is neither more or less than a "clearing house," a clearing house being a center where opinion is passed on checks, drafts, and accounts to determine whether they are valid and worthy of exchange. Somewhat similar to this, all souls, on leaving the body, pass to the soul world, there to await the time when they may be again permitted to take up the earth pilgrimage; this continues until the soul has finally attained Conscious Individuality, a Sonship with God, and can throw aside its carnality for Immortality.

All souls are granted the same opportunity; and endowed by their Creator with the powers and the faculties possessed by the Infinite; although these are in the beginning only potential, and must be gradually developed by *personal effort* to be available to man in attaining his highest estate; nevertheless, are capable of unfolding to such a degree that man will attain Conscious Individuality while in the flesh. Having achieved this through repeated earth pilgrimages, he will no longer have need of the soul realm through which to pass wherein to be tested respecting his fitness to use the potential forces with which he is endowed.

Though all souls are granted the same opportunity and endowed with divine powers, there is no Law in heaven or on earth forcing them to use these potentialities in the attainment of perfection. All are given free-will and right of choice; being at liberty to unfold, or to neglect, the Divinity within themselves. He who persistently neglects the Divine Image in which he is created, and wilfully and deliberately lives in ignorance, sin, and error through repeated opportunities on earth, will eventually forfeit the right to Conscious Individuality and Immortality. In other words, through repeated failure to comply with the necessary conditions for perfection, it is impossible for him to attain beyond animalism, because the *nucleus* of Divine potency within will remain in a state of dormancy. In the event of ultimate failure to comply with the terms of the Creator, the Spark of Divinity within, the Soul atom, unawakened to activity, returns in its original state, at the physical death of the body, to the universal storehouse of the Infinite.

Gradually, though admittedly slowly, individual Souls are attaining Consciousness. In so far as these Souls are concerned, there is no further need of the Soul World. What then?

That for which there is no further use, passes away; thus, ultimately, the soul world, "the first heaven," will cease to exist. It is this which John in his prophetic vision declares "was passed away." He forsaw the time when men would be taught a constructive philosophy, one enabling them to develop their fourfold nature, and attaining potential Manhood —a Conscious Individuality, and when the present heaven, the trial chamber of souls, would no longer be necessary.

What of the earth which he also saw "was passed away?" As with the first heaven, so with the first earth. As men attain perfection, so will the world and its conditions become ideal for existence. "The first earth" will have become "a new earth" and heaven and earth shall be one.

It is not at all difficult to comprehend that with the progress mankind generally is making toward individual unfoldment, economic conditions must likewise improve, and human relationships in every department of life become more desirable. The evolvement of souls on the earth manifests itself in improvement of humanitarian concerns and in the betterment of conditions on the social, industrial, educational, and governmental planes, is a truth already established in the race consciousness.

That this elevation of man in his fourfold nature has any effect upon the creatures of the earth who are less than man, or upon atmospheric, climatic, chemic, and other conditions to which man is subject, has as yet meagre claim in the race consciousness; is a truth that awaits man's recognition; is a part of the prophetic vision of "a new heaven and a new earth." That mankind has been given "dominion" over creation below him, and has the right and privilege to "subdue the earth," or to exercise his superior creative ability in improving the earth—is a truth that must become clearly outlined in the race consciousness before there can be a "new heaven and a new earth " That the passions, thoughts, emotions, and ideals of man affect the earth and determine its conditions as a dwelling place for men is a truth of which we are fully convinced; and is characteristic of the teachings of the new age; lying at the basis of a rational conception of Conscious Individuality.

Hermes, called the Thrice Wise, expressed an absolute law in a few words: "As above, so below." As above on the human plane, so below on the physical plane, both vegetable and animal. "As a man thinketh in his heart, so is he." Equally true, "as a man thinketh in his heart, so the animal world and vegetable kingdom about him." For every destructive passion and evil desire in the heart of man, there is apparent some evil or unfortunate manifestation in the external world. What man breathes out, animal and vegetable life breathes in and lives upon. Through the exhalations of his thoughts and passions, man furnishes food and nourishment to the kingdoms below him, both vegetable and animal. The breath of man is loaded with the vitality of his thought creations; if his thoughts are noble, pure and worthy, the emanations exhaled through his breath, being wholesome and vitalizing, feed and support the life of beautiful, valuable creations, as, flowers, herbs, birds, fowls, and animals of a superior order and beneficient character. If his thoughts and passions be destructive and ignoble, charged with ill-will toward others, the emanations exhaled through his breath are loaded with poisons, sustaining on planes below him life of an inferior order, or of a destructive and vicious nature; hence it is a literal fact "as above so below." As in the world of human thought and emotion, so in the world of manifestation in the subhuman.

These laws explain how man has dominion over the planes below him, and in truth is the creator and nourisher of kingdoms beneath. Neither is it a myth or fancy that awakening his soul into Conscious Individuality on the human plane is both the cause and creation of "a new heaven and a new earth." In proportion as man's thoughts and passions are exalted and pure, in like ratio are "the first heaven and first earth passed away." This throws new light on the mission of man; not only creator of his own destiny, not alone his "brother's keeper," but also in a very remarkable manner Lord of creation and master of both heaven and earth, and through thought, desire, emotion, and idealism, responsible for external conditions on the earth on which he lives; for realizing the Divine Purpose, by ushering in "the new heaven and the new earth."

Undesirable conditions on earth in its physical, as well as in its economic, industrial, and social features are due to the heavy, depressed, poisonous atmosphere emanating from man's thought world. Disasters resulting in loss of many lives; devastations and ravages by storm, flood, fire, and wind; violent wreckage of life through pestilence, drought and famine, and other dire calamities, unaccountable from physical causes merely, are recognized by the Seer as due to an excessive accumulation of poisonous vibrations from the realm of human thought and passion. If a fit of anger of the mother is powerful enough to poison the infant at her breast, inducing its death, how much more harm and disaster is spread broadcast by the accumulated poison of countless numbers of malicious and perverted lives. Argument is unnecessary to prove that mental states of an individual affect his physical condition. Sudden fright, sad news, prolonged uncertainty and anxiety, extreme violence of temper, intense fear, and other disturbed mental states, are fully recognized by all thinkers; and the skilful reasoning of scientist or psychologist is not required to convince man of the plausibility of the statement that mental conditions are often, very often, responsible for sickness and death, weakness and failure. If mental states are visibly effective in individual cases, how much more so must be the collective accumulation of a multitude of people. It is claimed by scientific investigators that all destructive passions, as, fear, anger, ill-will, malice, hate, melancholy, depression of spirit, form vibrations of heavy, solid, sluggish character, charged with poisonous elements and explosive substances. As thunder cloud meeting storm cloud results in an outburst of forces, liberating the destructive substances of each, so the collective cross-currents of thought and feeling emanating from many lives result in disaster and calamities, that are too frequently meekly accepted as "strange, but unaccountable visitations of Providence."

Remember that man and his soul, great as these are in the opinion of the egotist, are, in Biblical phraseology, said to be emanations from God. Man, being the prototype of God, also creates or destroys through his emanations.

Arguing constructively, if there is such power for harm in destructive mental emotions and passions, *how much greater the potency for good in constructive and righteous mental states?* Through the collective power of goodness, love, forgiveness, and justice emanating from the minds and hearts of many, conditions will so change as to make this earth a desirable habitation for Conscious souls. This will come about gradually and slowly, but eventually it shall be; it is actually now taking place; "the first earth" is in process of "passing away," "the new earth" in process of formation. To the Seer of the present day as to the Inspired Revelator of a former age, has been granted the prophetic vision of the "first earth" with its carnality, distress, and wreckage "passing away" and so fully convinced is he of the infinite power of Goodness operating through those reaching Conscious Individuality that he forsees the earth and its conditions becoming a fit dwelling place for "the redeemed of the Lord to walk thereon," that he is willing to give his life to the promulgation of the truth leading to this regeneration.

The philosophy of analogy reveals a correspondence, resemblance, or subtle kinship between life on the vegetable and animal kingdoms to human traits and characteristics. To illustrate: The serpent has always been considered symbolic of temptation, deception, and traitorous tendencies; the dove, of peace and good-will; the lamb, of innocence and gentleness; the lily, of purity and sinlessness; the rose, of beauty and perfection.

Are these emblematic interpretations merely a "happy coincidence?" Nothing more than observations which please and gratify the poetic and esthetic nature of man? Or is there a *fundamental reason, an eternal cause,* making them not only apt, but really vitally and universally significant?

The correctness and fitness of an analogy is testified to in the fact that it is accepted naturally and spontaneously by mankind generally. To point out an analogy is not the result of deep mental study or of careful reasoning; but of *soulful vision; a clear insight into fundamental truth.* If the association of qualities indicated by a symbol is true and accurate, the race consciousness accepts it spontaneously and without question.

With the seeker after truth it is different, he will not rest until he knows the reason "why." In time he discovers that there is a fundamental reason for the aptness of the analogy. To illustrate: The snake is emblematic of treachery and deceit. When the heart of man is filled with treacherous, deceitful, traitorous thoughts, desires, and motives, the exhalations of his breath are loaded with the particular poison that deceptive thoughts and purposes produce; this exhaled poison becomes the life and the sustaining force of the animal creation that corresponds to this type of thought. The deadly snake and poisonous viper are sustained and nourished by the destructive exhalations of perverted minds and darkened souls; and when men cease to have in their hearts the particular passions that the serpent represents and feeds upon, it will cease to exist; or, at least, it will no longer remain the creature loathed and abhorred by mankind almost universally, as at the present time. When man has finally overcome in his own nature the elements that the serpent represents, he ceases to have a marked abhorence to it; there is then nothing in his nature corresponding to it; and as an individual he no longer furnishes it life and nourishment; and though it may continue to exist, it will not be a terror to him. In proportion as the race evolves unto perfection of body, mind, and soul, in that degree will the serpent and deadly vipers, as well as all loathsome creeping, crawling creatures cease to exist as such; but will be transfigured creations, emblems fittingly representative of the graces and the virtues that have supplanted the destructive and deadly passions that previously existed in the hearts of men. *The serpent raised becomes the symbol of salvation, regeneration, or Conscious Individuality,* now, as like with Moses in the Wilderness, the *raising* of the Serpent making Health certain.

Thus all undesirable creatures on the animal plane will cease to exist when the thoughts of men are universally transmuted, and men universally entertain in their hearts only the divine passions of love, forgiveness, good-will, and other holy emotions, instead of the destructive and deadly thoughts of hate, malice, jealousy, envy, ill-will, and resentment.

In proportion as the race is redeemed and regenerated will the earth commence to abound in beautiful flowers, luscious fruits, and exquisite flying creatures. As men free their hearts of evil, deadly creatures and poisonous plants will disappear from the earth; in their stead coming flowers and creations infinitely more exquisite than man in his present unfoldment can possibly conceive in his imagination. So in time, the earth will become a Paradise, a veritable Garden of Eden; the men and women thereon gods and goddesses,—redeemed and perfected souls, but continuing to evolve new measurements and standards of perfection; still striving after ideals surpassing anything man is capable of comprehending.

Then man will be "lord of creation," enabled to "subdue the earth." Not merely by taming the fierce and vicious, is he to have dominion over the animal kingdoms, nor by destroying the ferocious and domesticating the wild; or by improving species; *but by living such a holy* (whole) *and sinless life that the emanations of his soul act as a redeeming and regenerating potency on the creation over which he has been made Lord and Master.*

The building of "a new heaven and a new earth" is the work of redemption, ceasing not with the salvation of humanity. Perfection of being is the goal and the ideal aimed at; but if man can see no farther than individual benefit, his aim is deficient or his desires largely selfish.

God is with men; He dwells with them; they are His people; but to come into a full realization of the kinship it is necessary that man obey the Law, both Natural and Divine, thus will he attain Conscious Individuality, Potential Power, Success, making Health certain.

Fraternally Given,
R. SWINBURNE CLYMER.

"Beverly Hall," Quakertown, Pa.
June 24, 1920.

Chapter One

Let the Sick Be Healed.

Jesus, whom multitudes recognize as one of the foremost exponents of the Divine Law, gave many admonitions to those who would follow the "Way, the Truth, and the Life;" irrespective of whether they believe him to have been divine. Of these none stands out more clearly than the command to heal the sick. In the Gospel of St. Luke are many references to the duty of the one to the other; the most direct and positive command is in verse nine of chapter ten:

"And heal the sick that are therein, and say unto them, The kingdom of God is come nigh unto you."

Why should the command: "Heal the sick," be accompanied by the statement that those who are healed shall be told the kingdom of God is come nigh unto them?

There is a close alliance between health and the kingdom of God; disease and the plane of error and sin. All illness is due to violation of the laws of health—and such disobedience to rules governing the well-being of man is error or sin; furthermore, those who commit sin cannot know heaven, for disease is pain and pain is purgatory or hell. The error or sin may be unconscious, nevertheless, "ignorance of the law excuses none," and all who disobey must pay the penalty to the "utmost farthing."

We freely concede that disease of body and mind is more often due to ignorance than to deliberate disobedience, but the ultimate result is the same. Where there is illness and suffering, there is neither ease nor harmony; a condition of discord is enthroned, heaven—a state of bliss—is unknown.

The command "heal the sick" should not be interpreted in its too literal sense, otherwise we would at once understand it as required of us to command the ill to "get up and walk." While this is possible in numerous instances, the real interpretation is, we should *instruct* all how to live; mentally, physically and spiritually, thus making a state of inharmony, or illness, impossible. This is what is meant by "Heal the sick."

The fact of a vital connection between health and the kingdom of heaven has been overlooked by most churches and religious denominations, or made a fetish of. The church has undoubtedly lost much of its hold upon humanity, largely because it has ceased to make healing of the bodily ills a prominent part of its mission. The New Commandment in its Christic Interpretations proposes to re-establish this important feature of religious instruction; and one of the essentials of the Humanitarian Society is to instruct and train its members in respect to natural laws as they pertain to physical and mental health, strength, and vigor, thus making Health certain.

This we consider to be an essential feature of the "Way, the Truth, and the Life," and under such instructions and training, every member should not alone regain health and strength, if lost, but also become qualified to help others in their search for health, for strength, and for vital stamnia, so necessary for success and happiness, which is the kingdom of heaven on earth.

This virile doctrine, that physical health and vigor are natural manifestations of the kingdom of heaven in human experience, while disease and suffering are symbolic of hades, or the sphere of error and darkness, is founded upon the Sacred Scriptures; and a basis for this may likewise be found in the ancient philosophies. It is actually not essential to use the Bible as authority; however, men generally recognize the teachings of the prophets and apostles recorded in the Bible as the foundation upon which all true doctrines rest; though there are some, indeed many, who consider themselves superior to all religious instructions; claiming they have no further need for philosophy and sacred writings; but this self-deluded superiority indicates they have not yet reached the first step on the

ladder of true Wisdom. All enlightened men recognize that
the Bible, whether they accept it as original or a rewriting of
ancient philosophies, contains the Alpha and Omega of all
knowledge, and that therein is clearly indicated the Way to
Life—the method for making Health certain. Therefore, the
Scriptural inculcations are accepted by us as the basis of our
instructions; acknowledging, at the same time, that the sacred
writings of other than the so-called Christian religion preserve
kindred doctrines.

We maintain that all illness, no matter what its nature,
is caused directly through refusal to live in harmony with the
Law of God, which Law has two aspects, one natural, the other
Divine. The Law of God, often designated as "the Law," or
"the Divine Law," is actually both natural and divine, but is
often spoken of as one or the other, due to the prominence of the
aspect in mind. In general, natural law refers to conditions on
the physical and material plane, and pertains to the physical
well-being of man; while divine law, variously considered, refers
to all things which affect the welfare of the soul, embracing the
mental, spiritual, and divine nature in man. There is, however,
no sharp distinction to be made between the two, because development of man's spiritual, mental, and divine nature actually
depends upon his physical well-being as a necessary basis. The
divine law rests upon the natural as a foundation; each is essential to the other; in fact, it is the same law viewed from
different angles.

Thus, let it be clearly understood in the beginning as a
basic proposition of the New Commandment; first, the state of
consciousness designated as "the kingdom of heaven" includes
right living (Righteousness), or correct habits of life, on the
physical plane, as well as in the spiritual, or divine, sphere of
thought; second; any consideration of the "Way, the Truth, and
the Life" that ignores the physical well-being of man is not only
incomplete, but irrational and illogical; third, the command to
heal the sick, is proof of the vital relation between health and
the kingdom of heaven, illness and the plane of sin and error,

makes it imperative for us to give instructions and training regarding the laws of health and formulate a rational basis and method for making Health certain.

It is the verdict of many physicians that illness is most frequently resultant in an erroneous system of living, or destructive habits of life; indeed, a more explicit statement would be: illness is most frequently induced by an inexcusably incorrect combination of food.

Time was, not many years agone, when it would have been thought absurd for a teacher, a prophet, or a Messiah, to associate dietetics with Life and with Salvation; but that age is past. In the present awakening, all wise men, all enlightened ones, know that all entering the body as food and drink has much to do with the welfare of it, therefore of the mind, consequently of the soul. The thoughtful person, of keen insight and normal mentality, no longer believes it irrational to associate hygiene and scientific dietetics with a life that makes Health certain.

In certain respects food and drink are to the body what oil is to machinery. A delicate mechanism may be thrown out of working order and rendered useless by being lubricated with a poor grade of oil; and not until it has been cleaned, reoiled, and its equilibrium re-established, will the machine satisfactorily serve the purpose for which it was intended. In like manner, man's organism may be thrown into a state of disorder and inharmony by ingesting food and drink unsuited for its requirements; and Health naturally impaired.

The stomach is the center of motive power of the entire organism*; and if that part of the human economy wherein constructive activity originates is reduced to inharmony and

---

*No less an authority than the great publisher Cyrus H. K. Curtis, of Philadelphia, writing for "Touchstones of Success" stated: "A sound physical condition depends upon what and how much you put *into* the body; and what and how much you take *out*, or in other words, perfect digestion and elimination. The whole secret of success starts right there—the treatment of the stomach. See to it that you get that right."

turmoil, the discord is transmitted to the brain through the medium of the sympathetic nerve, frequently causing unnatural and morbid thought and irrational action. Such destructive thought-action, in turn inducing sluggish, ambitionless movements of the body; and this physical inertia often accounting for inefficient workmen and artisans; and, in exaggerated form, may even be the basis of criminal tendencies or feeblemindedness. Futhermore, sluggish, congested, burdened and depressed physical functions largely explains the prevalent indifference among mankind to the Laws of Life, and the Salvation of all that is Immortal in man.

It is of equal importance to man to understand natural law as to be familiar with the divine, or spiritual law. Man is rightly called the prototype of the universe, or the microcosm; and, as such, he should understand the mechanism of his own physical structure and the method of its functioning, that he may abide by the dictates of universal order.

The church of the past has been inculcating the doctrine that souls alone are of value, and becoming immortal, or reaching salvation, regardless of physical conditions. Salvation of soul independent of the body is a dogma not sanctioned by the Christic Interpretation as it places a premium on weakness and physical slavery. Salvation by faith independent of works, or a manifestation of that faith, is not accepted by the New Commandment. Faith must be accompanied by works in harmony with the degree of the belief professed; full and perfect salvation of soul is impossible without a corresponding purification of the body; such are the definite tenets of the new, living, vital religious life of the new century; and there is every evidence that the Master teacher, Jesus, associated salvation of soul with health of body.

Possibly the strongest statement ever made by Jesus concerning the perfection of physical life, is:

"Whosoever liveth and believeth in me shall never die. Believest thou this?"

This, in the correct translation, would read: Whosoever believeth and *liveth* as *I teach,* shall never die. Contrary to the idea of multitudes, it is not sufficient to merely believe, irrespective of how sublime a truth may be, but requires actual obedience to the wisdom expressed. Science is daily proving the possibility of continual bodily rebuilding. It is a scientific fact that the physical body of man recreates itself entirely, cell by cell, within a period of nine months; and the only reason why the body becomes corrupted is because man does not live in harmony with the recreative law; some of the cells in the body being unable to renew themselves, remain to cause inharmony. This partial, instead of complete renewal, gradually induces age; or, in many cases, illness of the physical being, resulting in weakness of the mental and soul being.

Scientific research has proven conclusively there is no plausible reason why the body of man should become degenerate. What then is the remedy for the decrepitude of age and impaired physical conditions? Let the motto of the Christic Interpretation suffice for those who would make Health certain: "Our God is the God of life, not of death." Let the law as stated by St. John be the final answer to the question: "Whosoever believeth, and *liveth* in the Christ (true, or natural way) shall not die."

To live in the Christ is a natural sequence to true faith in all that Jesus taught. Jesus nowhere inculcated the doctrine that mere belief in the Christ would suffice; but distinctly stated that, whereby to attain Christhood, man must *live* as He lived—that is, in harmony with natural and divine law; only through correct living can man prove that he actually believes. Countless multitudes profess to have faith in God, but do not live in accordance with his commandments; and a faith that does not exemplify the Law is, at best, superficial; a self-deluded belief, swept away at the first indication of sorrow or trouble. To weep and to bewail one's fate, to wonder why man should suffer when, as he foolishly thinks, he trusts in the Lord—this very attitude of mind gives evidence of lack of faith which has its fountain in the heart. Implicit trust in God forces

one to a life in harmony with natural and divine law, are necessary supplements and companions, each of the other, making
Health certain.

All science and philosophy support the assertion that it
is impossible for a disordered mind resultant on a diseased
body, to have natural, simple, perfect faith and trust in either
man or the great Father. It is indeed contrary to reason to
believe that the mind can think correctly and to have clear
vision when it is depressed and morbid through physical disorder and congestion. On the contrary, when man lives in
harmony with natural and divine law, when he observes hygenic rules and honors the principles of right living on the
material plane as also on the mental and the divine, it is but
natural for him to have a wholesome and sincere trust in God,
the Father of all. The mind then receives none other than
cheerful, health-inspiring vibrations from the physical center in
the life of man; finding it easy to believe that there is a God; to
see the beauty in the rose; the harmony in the song of the
bird, and the glorification of God in Nature. All is bright and
desirable, the eye beholds the good and man is become like
unto the gods, thus is Health made certain.

Physical health, strength, and vigor characterize him in
whom "the kingdom of heaven is nigh at hand," disease and
disorder are symbolic of him in whom the darkness of sin and
error are reflected, are truths which both science and philosophy
support. Belief and trust will not be found missing in the
soul of the man who lives in harmony with both natural and
divine law.

The Laws of God pertain to life, and have reference to all
which form a part of daily living. It is well for man to give
careful attention to Regenerative precepts. No one should consider himself too wise, too far advanced, or too refined to become acquainted with the requirements for righteous living on
the physical plane. This includes sleep, labor, exercise, breathing, recreation, pleasures, cleanliness, a corrective diet and exalted thought habits. It is not uncommon for such who have

reached a certain degree of development to consider conditions which pertain to physical welfare of inferior significance; and be inclined to under-estimate the importance of the so-called commonplaces of daily life.

These should be reminded that the Bible is as much a text book on hygiene, sanitation, eugenics, and dietetics as it is a treatise on ethics, and the path to Salvation, or Immortality. Hygiene, sanitation, eugenics, and the importance of a correct diet vitally affecting salvation and immortality of body and soul. The fact that these all are a part of the life of man clearly indicates they are important enough to enlist his interest; and, if he really desires to attain health and peace, wisdom and happiness, he must, sooner or later, give heed to the natural law which governs the physical plane, thus Health becomes manifest, and happiness a certainty.

The superficial student seeking for a solution of reconstructive problems may smile at the emphasis placed on the importance of natural and hygienic laws; but, if sincere in his search, he need not look afar for ample proof of their importance. The fact that obedience to Nature's behests is essential, and that strict observances of all that pertains to sleep, work, exercise, recreation, breathing, food, and cleanliness is a necessary factor of an ennobling life, is not to be overlooked by any who would make life desirable and Health certain.

Concerning the command, "Heal the sick," it is to be remembered that, as illness is due to violation of the law in one or more of its aspects, so the restoration of the sufferer through a normal observance of the health rules violated, must be the aim. If illness is due to an incorrect dietary; disobedience of the laws of relaxation or sleep and rest; a lack of exercise; indifference to internal and external cleanliness; insufficient supply of pure air, or a combination of these indiscretions, restoration to complete health and harmony of the physical functions must include a rectification of all these errors.

An illustration of the results of refusing to live in harmony with the natural law in its various demands, note the serious and delusive ailment known as Neurasthenia, or Nerve Starvation. In most of these cases there is apparently not one indication of organic trouble, every organ and function may seem to be performing its duty; the physical being, to all appearance, and as far as examination will indicate, is normal.

But how is it with the mind and the soul of the sufferer? There is no sleep; or, if any, it is one horrible dream. There is no peace of mind; one morbid thought crowding out another; one delusion following the other. Though the sufferer attempts to control the mind, it is uncontrollable. The eyes cannot be closed for a moment unless panorama after panorama passes before the mental vision. He may look at the rose but can see no beauty in it. The sun may shine but to him there is no brightness. The vesture of field and woods have no charm for him. He contemplates life, but it is a waste of time. The Neurasthenic cares for neither beauty or love; life or death are as one to him. He cannot see a reason for his own existence, nor does he care whether there is heaven or hell after death. Life is a continuous horror to him, and those who have not suffered in like manner can form no adequate picture of such suffering.

It was of such cases as these that Jesus said they had a demon, or even many devils. The mind of the sufferer is one vast sphere of hallucinations. He knows these visions are delusions, are unreal; but lacking control, cannot cast them aside.

This is but a mild picture of a condition from which millions suffer in some degree; and multitudes rapidly approaching. It is asserted the white race is losing its "nerve," and gradually falling into this neurasthenic state.

What is the cause? The answer may seem absurd to many, but it is an absolute fact that starvation of the nervous system is responsible in most cases; this is due to long continued disobedience of the natural law in its various aspects—improper nourishment, hurry and rush in business, insufficiency of rest and sleep, lack of exercise and fresh air; chiefly because of the consumption of denatured food to the exclusion of Nature's offering.

And the Cure? The restoration of a person who has fallen into the clutches of this dread ailment must be along rational lines and include proper thought atmosphere, a correct dietary, plenty of exercise in pure air, sleep and rest, and encouragement. Even if it were possible to produce an instantaneous cure, of what value would it be if the one suffering were permitted to persist in former destructive habits? Nor must we forget that the Neurasthenic has lost faith in God; no longer believing in a future life; nor worrying a particle whether he possesses a soul or does not. Here we have a concrete instance of disease having a direct and profound influence on the mind and soul.

This serves merely as one illustration of the principle that in the restoration of health it is essential to communicate instructions dealing with the natural as well as the divine law; that the change in life must transform daily habits of living; that we must teach how to live as well as to believe in the Christ—to live a life of obedience to Nature's rule as well as to God's fiat; and trust, with sincerity and simplicity of heart, in God, the Father of all. Thus do we make Health certain and the goal is Happiness.

Chapter Two

*"And He sent them to Preach the Kingdom of God,
and to Heal the Sick."*

All who professed conversion to the religion inculcated by
Jesus were charged with a two-fold work: To preach the kingdom of God—pointing the way to an Elysian state of existence;
and, to heal the sick.

It is impossible to separate one from the other. Any attempt to do so ends in failure. The established churches have
been experimenting along this idea for centuries; but the many
attempted innovations are silent proof of their admission that
results have been far from satisfactory.

Many have questioned: Why should these two departments of work go hand in hand—"to preach the kingdom of God,
and to heal the sick?" It would be more pertinent and rational
to ask: Why should not these two services, preaching the kingdom and *pointing the way to health, go hand in hand?* Why
should they ever have been separated at all, understanding as
we do, that to find the kingdom is likewise to have made Health
certain.

Their separation was due to an erroneous interpretation of
the phrase "the kingdom of heaven,'" a mistaken idea of the
relation existing between soul and body; a misconception of the
meaning of the words "salvation" and "redemption." Undoubtedly their reunion will be effected through the acceptation of
the Christic Interpretation of the kingdom of God and its relation to man in *every* department of his life.

According to the Christic Interpretation, the kingdom of
God includes the domain of health and right living on the physical plane; the salvation of the soul cannot be separated from the

regeneration of the body; redemption of soul pre-supposes rejuvenation of body; Life and Regeneration, in its full and complete realization, anticipates ultimate victory over weakness and
sickness and the terror of the grave. When the truth concerning
man and his relationship to God is finally comprehended, man
living the natural life, realizing this ideal existing between
himself and the Creator, illness will be impossible.

"Whosoever liveth, and believeth in the Christ shall never
die."

Here again we meet two principles which must not be separated; but must go hand in hand,—living and believing. He
who lacks faith will refuse to live the life of the faithful; while
he who trusts in the supremacy of the law will live accordingly
and will reap the benefit of his credence; the fruits of which
are freedom from disease and weakness, and the possession of
Happiness.

"Christ" is not supposed to refer to a personality, but to a
state of being. Such as live the Regenerative life will develop
within themselves the Conscious Soul, or Conscious Individuality,
and this is a Christ. These shall never die because they have,
in the present incarnation, established their relationship with the
Father. Moreover, such will have arisen above many of the
weaknesses of the flesh, will be immune from disease, and have
made Health certain.

Let it be remembered that the promises throughout Sacred
literature of a never-ending life are only to those who live in
the Christ and believe in Him. To those who do not so live,
who are not in harmony with His laws, no such promise is offered; neither are such capable of entertaining a correct conception of the principles of Conscious Individuality. Only to
the sense enslaved, carnal pleasure loving nature is the promise
of Regeneration uninviting. To those who have tasted of the
goodness of the kingdom, who have but partially realized the
power and the beauty of the life in Christ, the assurance of Immortality as an ideal possible of attainment, is worth laboring
for; and they fully comprehend that its realization can come

only through obedience to the Divine law and faith in the existence of the Christ-Principle in humanity.

The New Commandment aims at re-establishing the vital and essential correspondence between the kingdom of God and the principles underlying health. It advocates the practical union of preaching this kingdom and making Health certain.

It cannot be too strongly impressed upon all who would represent the new Age and its constructive doctrines, that they must become teachers of health as well as enlightened instructors in the Divine Law. They must be inculcators of the truth as interpreting a continuous and uninterrupted existence, first here, and then in a Soul sphere; devotees of a rational life which accepts the advocation of the tenet that physical well-being is of equal importance with salvation of soul.

Among people generally, there is a grievous misconception concerning the ministry of the Master Jesus. Multitudes still belive he healed the sick despite their sinful life; and that they retained health though they did not denounce their old life of sin. Such a conception of the mission of Jesus is far from the truth and is delusive; in each instance of which we have record, he tested the faith of those who came to him for help; and, when he found it satisfactory, gave them of his best, but always with warning that they should sin no more, indicating thereby that he had instructed them in the ways of righteousness (right living) beforehand, otherwise his admonition of "go thy way and sin no more" would have been meaningless.

Jesus fully comprehended the logic that health and harmony (health *is* harmony) cannot exist in the body of one who continues in deliberate, persistent wrong doing (sin), and especially the particular error which was the basic cause of the sickness. To attempt freeing one of disease while ignoring the cause and permitting him to continue in habits that foster disease, is both irrational and contrary to divine authority; nor is there the slightest basis for such an interpretation of the cases where health was restored to those suffering.

Doubtless the greater reason for testing the faith of those

who came to him was to determine whether the sufferer understood the laws governing health and showed a willingness to seek freedom from the cause of the trouble. The faith that does not include a desire to give up habits of life which induce illness of body or mind, is irrational. The credence that expects to be relieved from illness regardless of cause, and to remain well despite unnatural and abnormal habits of life, is deficient of understanding; not based on either natural or divine law; and shames every law of honor and justice. To believe that Jesus or any other instantaneously healed the body of man without enlightening the sufferer how to avoid like difficulties in the future, is to make of him a mere wonder-worker and charlatan.

The mission of the Humanitarian Society is to teach the clearly indicated laws of life; how to live and what to believe, whereby man may become healthy, strong, and efficient (successful). It is an exceedingly practical one; there is no misconception permitted that its instructions deal only with the so-called spiritual or unseen, and, consequently, with theories impractical and fanciful. The purpose of the New Commandment, in its various interpretations, is to make its teachings regarding the Law that leads to a fuller Life and a Conscious Individuality, applicable to every-day needs; and there is nothing more necessary today amongst mankind than health, strength, efficiency and a clearly defined philosophy of Redemption and Rejuvenation. No mission can be more exalted and practical than that of teaching the laws of God concerning man's Immortal self, in conjunction with the making of Health certain.

This is the New Age, the era in which man must understand that religion is not merely a combination of peculiar ideas to be accepted and believed without question; but the *revelation of a mode of life,* one that can be, and must be, lived daily. As a revelation of the laws of life, it includes every department of man's nature, and is, therefore, not a theory, but a practical working monitor which is satisfying to the daily requirements of life *here and now.*

The end and aim of the life of man is to become like unto

the gods. Being endowed with divine potentialities and deific attributes and powers, he fulfills his mission in proportion as he develops his forces in harmony with universal law and order. When man lives entirely within the law, naturally and normally, he will be free from illness, from corruption, and from everything undesirable; becoming gradually like unto the gods and fully conscious of his Oneness with the Infinite. Sin and sickness, corruption and age, no longer are part of his nature. Admittedly these statements picture an ideal state; and men generally are incapable at the present moment of realizing this; but to sense the ideal and the possibility of its attainment, is essential as a stimulus to urge one to even a partial realization, and in proportion as desire urges obedience and effort, will be the ultimate achievement.

To live the life of the Christ does not mean, as formerly interpreted by the religious denominations, merely the redemption of the spiritual part of man; that idea was abandoned under the light of understanding that characterizes the present age. The Christic Interpretation maintains that redemption concerns the body of man equally with the soul, that salvation—literally, "a making sound, safe, and whole"—pertains not merely to the soul, but likewise to the body. The more faultless the soul, the more exquisite will be its reflection in the body; and, under normal conditions, according to the perfection of the body, will be the flawlessness of the soul. However, external appearances are not always a reliable index; the physique may be apparently ideal, and yet there may be an internal cancer that is gnawing away the life of the body and soul. To live the life of the Christ refers to true perfection of body and soul; the soul which has become enlightened through love, wisdom, and understanding, and is on the path to Deific Consciousness,—the body that directs its forces into channels of etheralization and Conscious Individualization—this pictures the actual meaning of living the Christ life.

A vital lesson for the seeker to comprehend is that the body is of utmost importance in the work of soul development; that physical perfection greatly helps, indeed, is necessary, in the attainment of soul illumination; that the two—physical culture, aiming at health, strength, and success, and soul awakening, visualizing the development of deific powers and exalted consciousness—must be equal and harmonious. If the aspirant possesses wisdom, he will exercise scrupulous care regarding the requirements of the body in every respect, whereby it may become a greater help and a stronger support to him in his efforts toward advancement in both the material and spiritual realms.

The student may learn a lesson from the experience of the foolish virgins. He will be careful to not only have a sufficiency of oil for his vessel,, but have it of superior quality; giving thoughtful consideration to the amount and quality of food and drink taken for nourishment; consuming only such as will give him strength and vitality; avoiding that class and those combinations which might induce illness or weakness. He realizes that strength, vigor, and vitality of the body is the basic foundation for soul supremacy and his legitimate right to inheritance of the kingdom. He must fully comprehend that perfection of body aims at continual, daily transmutation and renewal of cells and the changing of the old into finer and of more spiritual quality; this continuous transfiguration of the physical into a higher and more exalted type tending constantly toward the immortalization of both body and soul, and is the process of making Health certain.

Religious propagandists of the past were active and zealous in their tirades against the use of intoxicants of every description; this was to be commended; but the New Commandment proceeds much farther than this; it recognizes that other drinks than those termed intoxicants, are injurious and therefore to be condemned; that inferior quality of food and incorrect combinations thereof are productive of positive harm-producing illness and inducing crime through the effect upon the nervous system and the brain. We further maintain that unwise selections of non-nutritious foods and their combination definitely affect the growth and the purity of man's spiritual being. Many are vitriolic in their condemnation of spirituous liquors, who are indifferent to the degenerating effects of so-called "soft" drinks; likewise ignorant of the fact that an excess of tea, coffee, and other common beverages acts as poison to the system as truly as do the malted and refined liquors.

It is desirable that all should know wine to be "a mocker and strong drink raging;" but it is *more* important to realize that other drinks common among men and believed to be harmless, are nerve-wrecking, morality-shattering, and soul-destroying; because a greater number enjoy them, and they have their most harmful influence upon children who have not attained full bodily growth, nor developed moral strength; likewise upon countless women who are to become mothers.

It is equally essential for all to possess the knowledge than an excess of certain food elements and a deficiency of other elements is the direct cause of many of the ailments which afflict man and that, by merely rectifying these excesses and deficiencies, the sufferer may be restored to normal; this is God's way of "healing the Sick" and making Health certain.

In a much greater degree than is generally supposed, health, strength, efficiency, *and* morality, is the result of proper nourishment*. Certain elements are demanded by the human body wherewith to keep it physically fit. In the selection of food, it is not sufficient to give the one item of nutrition attention, but the correctness of proportion of necessary constituents and the har-

---

*See the book "Diet, The Way to Health,"

monious combination of them, must be considered. Health cannot be certain as long as man is ignorant of the food requirements of his body.

The Christic Interpretation maintains that its position is
sane and logical in claiming that food and drink are legitimate
subjects of attention for those who are truly and deeply inter-
ested in the kingdom of heaven and in the restoration of those
not in possession of health. It is on a firm foundation of reason
and practical experience in making the claim that full and complete salvation of soul is impossible in a body that is under-
nourished, racked by starved and sensitive nerves, or poisoned
by secretions of dead material. If Religion has a right to condemn a liquor which intoxicates and by its influence on the
brain, induces a man to commit crime, it *must* be equally just to
condemn food, or a combination thereof, which through congestion, produces depression of the nerve and brain centers, thus
exciting to crime. If one has its influence on the soul, then the
other certainly has, and must receive equal condemnation.

In acceptance of the command to preach the kingdom of
God, and to heal the sick, we consider it our mission to place
proper emphasis upon the intimate and vital relation existing
between soul and body. The laws of life as they pertain to
hygiene and the correct care of the physical being, are as much
a feature of the kingdom as pure thoughts and lofty aspirations. To live and to believe in Christ, in its full and comprehensive interpretation, includes a knowledge of, and obedience
to, natural law in its relation to man's physical welfare.

Many who come to us for help and advice have considered
the life advocated by us as too exacting for them. Possibly
after a partial, half-hearted trial, some will return to the old,
death-dealing life; in doing so, they take upon themselves the

old weaknesses and disease, often in exaggerated form. The undesirable effects of the old life are a thousand times harder to endure than would be the denial of a few destructive habits which cause the difficulties, if only sufficient strength were husbanded to overcome them. Nothing but whole-hearted loyalty and sympathetic devotion to the principles of life on both the physical and mental plane can be accepted as a fair and honest test of the life which makes Health certain.

It would be delusive to believe that the new life advocated by the Christic Interpretation is painfully exacting and difficult to follow; rather, the reverse is true. The results are so beneficial that it quickly becomes a delight to perfect oneself in the practice of its precepts. Often a few simple changes in the daily routine will be all that is necessary to effect a satisfactory restoration to health, strength, and success. A few non-essential items, which would never have been indulged were it not for erroneous teachings, may need to be eliminated; but the cross these principles impose is not hard to bear; it denies man nothing that gives elevating pleasure, or proving of benefit to him; prohibiting only that which gives slight, temporary enjoyment of short duration, followed by great pain or sorrow.

The New Commandment teaches a system of normal, natural living as regards habits which affect physical health and spiritual illumination; a philosophy that promotes elevating thought and right action in the individual life. Its purpose is to touch the mainspring of thought and motive, and to lift the standard of incentive to the plane of Light and Life, away from that of disease, failure, and death. It instills into the ill and unfortunate the conviction that man must live correctly if he would be free from disease, suffering, and failure; that through obedience he may master and possess all that is truly desirable and worth while .When the seeker for help fully realizes this, the Teacher-Healer can effectively say to him: "Thy sins be forgiven thee, go thy way and sin no more," and thus it shall be; for marvelous is the power entrusted to those who obey the will of God.

When man persists in thinking elevating thoughts, in encouraging refining emotions, and in correct habits of life, he will find that mortality passes into immortality; that the bodily cells are daily being transmuted into cells of finer quality. He who liveth and thinketh in the Christ will gradually become more and more like Him. This is the promise of the Father, the Giver of Life, to mankind, not only through Jesus, who became the Christ by following the doctrine he taught, but through all the great masters and philosophers of the past ages.

"God is the giver of life and not of death," must be resounded throughout the universe; and those who suffer in body, in mind, and in soul, must be enlightened so that they may partake more of life, and less of that which belongs to death; for let it be understood that weakness, illness, disease, inefficiency, instability, failure, all these belong, not to life, but to death.

Were it untrue that the body of man is of value, and in need to be exalted and honored with immortality, God, the Father of all, and His messengers would never have called it the Temple of the Soul, or the Temple of the Living God. That the Soul may be perfect, the temple must be made pure and holy, and be honored with irreproachable care. This is possible by having confidence in the promise given by God to man and by living in harmony with the laws of idealism. He who so believes and lives, is daily attaining; it cannot be otherwise, for he is complying with the necessary requisites in the achievement of ultimate Conscious Individuality.

Our God is the "God of Life and not of death," and promises that man shall not taste of death if he lives and believes; but He also says with equal emphasis, "the soul that sinneth it shall die." Likewise is it a truth that the body that sinneth, and exists not in harmony with natural and divine law as exemplified by the Christ, shall be full of disease and sorrow. This is not because God desires it to be so, or arbitrarily wills it, because the violation of the law *automatically brings its own penalty*. He who transgresses the law of harmony suffers the inconvenience of inharmony; he who disobeys the edict of order must suffer the natural consequences of disorder; he who transgresses the rules pertaining to health, must endure illness and failure; while he who lives in harmony with universal law and order, will reap the benefits of peace and harmony, and he who willingly pays the price of life and immortality will obtain the blessings of health and success; and all who live and believe in the Christ (the Divine in all created things) pass from mortality to immortality; for these there is no death.

Our Mission

The mission of the Humanitarian Society is to teach the clearly indicated laws of life; how to live and what to believe, whereby man may become healthy, strong, and efficient (successful). It is an exceedingly practical one; there is no misconception permitted that its instructions deal only with the so-called spiritual or unseen, and, consequently, with theories impractical and fanciful. The purpose of the New Commandment, in its various interpretations, is to make its teachings regarding the Law that leads to a fuller Life and a Conscious Individuality, applicable to every-day needs; and there is nothing more necessary today amongst mankind than health, strength, efficiency and a clearly defined philosophy of Redemption and Rejuvenation. No mission can be more exalted and practical than that of teaching the laws of God concerning man's Immortal self, in conjunction with the making of Health certain.

Chapter Three

Believe in Life and Live. Accept the Doctrine of Death and You Will Surely Die.

Throughout the ages, humanity generally, not excluding even the fathers of the Church, has believed in a God of death; considering sickness and suffering as the natural inheritance of man; hence the entire race has been inoculated with the conviction that disease and death are unavoidable. This certainly appears unreasonable, the Master teacher Jesus clearly indicating throughout his entire ministry, that whosoever believes and lives in the Christ (the true life) shall not die.

The virile doctrine promulgated by the master teacher positively declares that illness and death have no part in the life of the true man; therefore, should not be included in his Faith; yet man is only now awakening to the fact that he has been grossly guilty of serious mistakes these many years. He is gradually arriving at the conviction that instead of having had faith in Life and Immortality—a God of Life and Happiness, he has given habitation in his heart and mind to the ancient race belief in the necessity of disease and suffering,—a god of death; in mortality rather than Immortality.

This race belief in the necessity, or the impossibility of avoiding disease, has acted as a slow, death-dealing poison, a virus inoculating Man's entire being; bringing upon him these very conditions; thereby burdening him with weakness and failure, the end whereof is death.

But the epoch of spiritual darkness is passing, while the cycle of wisdom and understanding is being rapidly ushered in. With the birth of the new age, and the understanding of the Christic Interpretation which consistently advocates a God of life as opposed to one of death, the changing of the belief in mortality to one in Immortality; while for the old doctrine inculcating the idea that man is "a worm of the dust," it substitues the logical one that he is actually " a child of the King," a creation of God the Father, whose rightful inheritance is Immortality and Conscious Individuality. The New Commandment is doing all in its power to break the chains of bondage to the credence that disease and death are man's inevitable heritage, and maintains firmly and openly the conviction that man's destiny is to become like unto God, the Father, his Creator; that it is his mission to express the Divine character and attributes, to exemplify his Divine possibilities, thus finding happiness and securing power, and making Health certain.

We Command you: Tear from the heart of you the age-old idea that man must forever suffer and be in sorrow. Establish in your soul and mind an active faith in the possibility of continued health and of attaining ultimate Immortality. Break the fetters that bind you to the race belief in the necessity of sin and death. Live simply, naturally, and normally, in accordance with Nature's and God's Law; and you will shortly free yourself from disease and weakness, from sorrow and failure, and ultimately from the fear of death. This is the doctrine inculcated by the Humanitarians in the New Commandment, and is making Health certain.

Not alone is it essential to cast aside forever the race belief in the necessity of disease, sorrow and failure; but also to attain an active, abiding faith in the power and the reliability of the All Father, and in His promises that man may possess health and happiness, and become as one of the gods. It is likewise of the utmost importance for man to live in harmony with such a professed faith and cultivate habits exemplifying it.

The mode of life daily manifesting a perfect reliance in the All Father includes all that affects man's physical welfare, such as, sleep, rest, exercise, work, and thought. Worry, haste, anxiety, hatred, malice resentment and fear are destructive and must be eliminated from mind and heart. The one seeking to personify the true life must honor the laws of Nature as they pertain to the elements, as air, light and sunshine; must so arrange his interests as to apportion his time between active work, rest and relaxation, exercise and innocent pleasures, including all that under normal conditions, brings health and happiness to man.

The seeker for the highest that life has to offer must guard against those elements in food which are not conducive to his welfare in every respect. Perhaps there is no other habit more detrimental to health than the over-indulgence in sweets and starches to the exclusion of the essential nerve-and-vitality-building foods. If we ingest an excess of sweets and starchy elements, it is utterly impossible to consume the required amount of the vital food with which the system must be supplied, resulting in disease, age, failure, and death; respecting drinks, we must learn to avoid those which are stimulating, and indulge freely in those which are eliminating and thirst quenching. If these suggestions are rationally observed, balance, or harmonious adjustment of forces obtains; this is conducive to efficiency, youth, long life, making Health certain.

Under present economic conditions, with the exception of

the hard working manual laborer, man should deny himself
almost entirely the starchy foods, especially the white, denatured
breads and pastry; these are disease inducing and death dealing. We include too great an amount of refined sugars; they rob
the system of the natural lime necessary to its well-being, and
create an abnormal craving for tea, coffee, and other stimulating
drinks. Man imagines he requires these apparent foods, and
indulges freely, to find in them superficial and merely temporary
effects, and of no vital, permanent value to human economy.
When the correct dietary is adhered to, the unnatural desire
for stimulants and an over-abundance of food gradually di-
minishes, and an actual rebuilding of the system eventually taking place; the entire organism is liberated from those serums
inducing illness, weakness, inefficiency, age, and Health results.

The Christic Interpretation considers not alone the soul,
but also the physical man; fully comprehending that the Immortal Soul must have its foundation in a normal, healthy habitation; without the material vehicle through which to manifest,
the soul cannot develop permanency of individual existence.
The New Commandment recognizes the whole (holy) being;
in this, it harmonizes with the Great Teacher, as also with the
wise old philosophers, in their emphasis on Life and Immortality, and *an active faith which manifests in works.*

The religion advocated by the New Commandment is not a
fanatical faith, but one founded on reason and truth. It is
practical results which verify the truth or the falsity, the benefit
or the disadvantage, of a system or doctrine. The Christic
Interpretation has been satisfactorily tested time and again
and proves beyond dispute, that when man *obeys* the principles
inculcated and offers them a thorough, faithful trial, in every

instance health, peace, efficiency, and success were resultant fruits. Through these the Humanitarians are becoming daily more zealous in the propagation of the principles taught; firmly convinced that theirs is a normal, rational faith, a wisdom based on the correct interpretation of Truth.

The ancient precept has been that the chief aim and end of life is "to glorify God, and to enjoy oneself forever." When one seriously considers the meaning of the expression, "to glorify God," it must be admitted that it is all-inclusive in its scope; that it may well be regarded as the "chief end and aim of life." Alas! How few give these words any serious thought.

How better can man possibly glorify God than by becoming like Him, by living the natural, normal, happy life whereby to free himself from the burden of illness, suffering, and sorrow? How better, than by being able to say: "Here am I, my body is perfect, functioning as freely and as regularly as the universe, part of which I am. Here I stand, not merely whole of body, but with a soul ideal in its activities. My physical being is like the universe in its obedience to law and order. My soul like the Father who rules the universe. Though but a miniature being, a Macrocosm, I am fashioned after the great universe, the Macrocosm; and my Soul daily inhales of the perfection of the Father. I obey, to the best of my ability and understanding, the command, 'Be ye therefore perfect even as your Father in heaven is perfect.' "

However extravagantly imaginative these words may appear to the sense-bound, carnal mind, there is nothing of sacrilege or blasphemy in them. They merely express obedience to the standard as taught by Jesus after becoming the perfect Soul, the Christ, through obedience to the laws he taught. When properly understood, they express the deepest humility man can comprehend; the most complete self-renunciation; the most profound sincerity and simplicity of trust in God, the Father, rather than in the self.

In manifesting such a degree of development, man is no less a *man;* and it is then that he enjoys himself forever; he is not required to give up anything which can possibly give him enjoyment or true happiness. He must refuse only that bringing him temporary pleasure, and which, like a thief of the night, is robbing him of tenfold more than it is offering. No seeker need fear he will be called upon to denounce any joy belonging to the normal human being; such is not true. That which may result in pain or sorrow to the one indulging or to another is always forbidden man; it is deceiving and destructive. It is well to accept the principle that the chief end of life is to glorify God and to enjoy oneself forever; but it must be borne in mind joy is illegitimate when it is at the expense of the self or of any other.

Under bondage of the old race belief that sickness cannot be avoided, that man is born to suffering, death ending all, there could be no certain lasting pleasure; for in the midst of it the thought of illness and death would creep in. Under the new dispensation, all this proved untrue; and man *learns* he need *not* "surely die," but may "surely live," if he is willing to obey the law and live the Christ life, thereby making Health certain.

Nor is this all. In obtaining freedom for the physical being, the Temple, there is likewise created something infinitely greater—the awakening of the Soul, the evolution of Conscious Individuality. It is here the Christic Interpretation finds its strongest basis for faith in the Fatherhood of God and the Immortality of the Soul; because, as man obeys both natural and divine law; as he obtains freedom for the body, he liberates the soul which has been bound as with chains of steel. Through continually living the Christic life, the soul is born anew; and will comprehend many things unknown to mere physical man. In consequence of this manifold development, man becomes, in truth, like one of the Gods; a clear vision of the object of life, with power and success, as his reward.

The soul in man is constantly striving for liberty and enlightenment; it has been seeking freedom from bondage, lo, these many years; but physical man has been unable to free himself from the race belief, and until his mind can cast aside the shackles, the spirit cannot manifest. The universal race conviction has been gripping mankind almost universally in unelastic bonds, and causing men individually to shrink in horror from thinking for themselves and accepting a doctrine not favored by the masses. But the universal soul is becoming superior to its environments; the destructive belief in the necessity of disease and senility, is broken; the new cycle and spiritual dispensation has brought in a new era; a time has come wherein man shall no longer fear to think, to plan, to achieve, and to cast aside the shackles which made him well nigh helpless. Man is gradually learning to conquer his ancient enemy, making Health certain.

We have been laboring these many years, teaching that the soul of man is immortal; that his body may be brought to a refinement free from corruption; and that all may draw upon the universal spirit of God as freely and fully as they choose and thus obtain life more abundantly. Teachers and Philosophers have been doing their best to point us "the Way, the Truth and the Life;" that few actually understood, is apparent in the fact that on all sides abounds misery and sorrow, disease and corruption; vast multitudes still believing that only in death

are peace and contentment found. The masses have either forgotten, or never fully comprehended, that knowledge brings life
more abundantly; that understanding of natural law is as
bread from heaven; while they who partake freely shall find life
and not death. Mankind has been blind these many centuries;
unable to accept the tenet that life and not death, joy and not
sorrow, health and not disease, may be the common lot of man.

That the end and aim of life is to glorify God and to exemplify the principle that God is the God of life and not of
death, we have been inculcating consistently for many years. It
is a truth pure and uncontradictable; given as it came to us from
the fountain of knowledge. It is not offered in symbolism and
obscure phraseology, that only the few can comprehend, but in
language clear and easily understood, that all may grasp the
meaning, live the life, and reap the fruits.

Learn to know the truth, then live according to the truth.
Believe actively that the life of the Christ (Nature and God) is
good; that man is *not* born to suffering and disease; nor need
he be a creature of pain and misery if he is willing to comply
with the natural and divine law. Let each one live in harmony
with the truth that man is made in the image of the Creator,
God; casting aside forever the thought that he must suffer and
"surely die." Instill in its place the conviction that you are a
child of the Father, who has given you all power; that sin and
sickness are not for you, but instead, more and continually more
of life are yours, ending in Conscious Individuality or Immortality.

Free yourself from the shackles of the race belief in the
necessity of sin, disease, and failure; this belief attracts the objects of its faith and tends toward conditions the thought represents. *Comprehend* that God is good, and in the Universal

Storehouse of God is life; free and abundant wherefrom you may draw according to your requirements. The only requisite enabling you to receive from the Infinite Storehouse the vibrations of life and success, is a faith sufficiently strong in God and yourself, enabling you to live a normal, natural life, one free from destructive thoughts and acts. This is making Health certain.

We gladly teach the humble seeker these truths: How to live; how to draw upon the Infinite Supply of Life, of Love, and of Wisdom; how to harmonize the personal self with the Universal Law, thereby obtaining freedom from disease, suffering, and other undesirable conditions. Faith is the beginning of new life; and works must follow that trust; the desire must be to the end to be achieved; and, as a consequence of constructive thoughts, correct belief, worthy and exalted desire, life will be in harmony with the Universal Law, and eventually, mortality will be refined into Immortality, man realizes Conscious Individuality, Health and happiness are certain.

The Creative Life

The virile doctrine promulgated by the master teacher positively declares that illness and death have no part in the life of the true man; therefore, should not be included in his Faith; yet man is only now awakening to the fact that he has been grossly guilty of serious mistakes these many years. He is gradually arriving at the conviction that instead of having had faith in Life and Immortality—a God of Life and Happiness, he has given habitation in his heart and mind to the ancient race belief in the necessity of disease and suffering,—a god of death; in mortality rather than Immortality.

Chapter Four

God's Plan is the Deathless Life

In permitting the Divine Spark to leave the Emphyrean spheres and incarnate in a physical, or material, body on the earth plane, it was God's plan that, first, through incarnation, the embryonic soul would become a personality, separate from God, the All Creator; second, this personality, through development, should attain Conscious Individuality; a self-existence separate from the Creator.

By the attainment of personality and of individuality, the soul spark is destined to pass through experiences giving it the knowledge of good and evil, pain and sorrow; though it was not the divine plan it should stop when this wisdom had been obtained. On the contrary, the soul was to pass onward and upward until it had reached the Sublime Realization, or Sonship with the Father, termed the Illumination.

Between the man who is merely a personality and the one who has attained individuality, there is a mighty gulf. The one is of the flesh and lives accordingly. He may believe in God, but he does not *know* God; he is a carnal being with worldly desires, and, at best, is little more than "a worm of the dust." He has but slight comprehension of the divine possibilities latent in himself; his aspiration for higher and greater achievement is truly meagre; he has not yet actually awakened from his long earthly sleep which followed the "fall" of the soul into the habitation of flesh with its native passions. Far different is the man who has achieved individuality; he has awakened to the real meaning of those principles taught by Jesus and all other great masters before him. He is filled with a burning aspiration to live in harmony with the law, and to test the highest standards of life; his ambitions are for true development of all that is best in him. He longs for a full and exalted consciousness of his own Oneness with the Infinite. Through lofty and worthy aspirations, and a life of self sacrifice and usefulness to others, he arouses the Fire, the Soul, within his own being, into a state of watchfulness and dynamic activity; and thereby the Flame of the Soul gradually develops into the Christos, a Son of God.

Moreover, in the full realization of this Christos, the individual can comprehend the significance of the promise, that the last enemy to be overcome, is death. He will understand that this assurance may actually consummate; furthermore, he will gain the knowledge *how* the covenant is to be fulfilled; perceiving that it is possible for the time to come when man shall no longer be sick and in sorrow; that in the final awakening of the Christos, he becomes truly conscious of his Sonship with the Father—the Dove of Peace descends upon him, and, in an unmistakable voice, proclaims: "This is my beloved Son in whom I am well pleased."

This is the Sublime Realization; it is the aim and the end of man's life on earth. It is the purpose and the plan of the Creator, the Heavenly Father, that *all* men should finally reach this inheritance. In infinite wisdom, God has endowed man with free-will and the right of choice; he is therefore at liberty to accept or to reject "the Way, the Truth, and the Life" that leads to this exalted Consciousness.

Two possibilities are placed before man, subject to his choice of action. The one opens to him the opportunity of unfolding his divine nature and developing his deific attributes, exemplifying the fact that he is created in the Divine image, and leading to the attainment of Conscious Individuality, Sonship with the Father. It is the path often of self-crucifixion and of final sublime exaltation; is marked by purity of thought and purpose; a continual surrender of the carnal nature to the Exalted Ideal, a perpetual transmutation of the baser metals (passions) of the lower personality, into the pure gold of spirituality. It is the awakening of the soul, which culminates in an Immortal Individuality; its chief seals are goodness and service to others. If man does not, of his own free choice, travel this path and meet the full requirement of its conditions, he pays the penalty of retrogression; and the Divine Spark of a soul smoulders under the ashes of selfishness and carnality. Persisting in deliberate sin and destructive habits, he will eventually be cast back to the elements whence he came. This Flame, once part of God, having failed to attain Conscious Individuality, returns to the Father, losing its identity in the storehouse of universal essence; while the body returns to mother earth which gave it birth.

The end and goal of life is consummated in Conscious Individuality, or Oneness with God. This, both in the process of attainment and in the final realization, is a life of service to humanity; it is a life of faith, attended by constructive work.

The average man does not really believe the promises God gave; he considers himself convinced; but his life proves he is far from confident of the fulfillment. If he actually gave credence to the covenant, he would live in accordance with the law; would be loyal in his services and not continually harassed by illness, pain and sorrow. The suffering of the multitudes round about us clearly indicate that men generally have little faith in God or in His promises and this we would remedy, making Health certain.

The first step to be taken in the search for freedom from all undesirable conditions is for man to instil in his own heart faith in the absoluteness of the Universal Law. It is immaterial whether this is accomplished through acceptation of the promises given in the Sacred Scriptures or the teachings of the old philosophers. Having accepted, he must prove his faith by practice; as he lives the life, he *will reap the reward of life.* The results will show greater knowledge; which increases as his faith becomes stronger. Man must use the one talent he possesses, doing so, others will be given him, until finally all the talents will be his; such is the promise.

In the hearts of all men there is a divine impulse, one the multitudes scarcely recognize; this is constantly operative, day and night, year in and year out, and being misunderstood, frequently incites man to commit deeds which are destructive. Such an impelling force was implanted in the heart of man by his Creator as the incentive compelling him to seek for wisdom; for strength to succeed, until finally Conscious Individuality is attained.

If man will listen to this Voice within and heed its intimations, it will lead him ever upwards and onwards; and as he follows the one impulse to consummation, another will take its place. Thus, step by step, he is led toward the final Realization, and in proportion as he becomes conscious of it, will he experience health, happiness and success. As he substitutes in place of the race belief in the unconquerable universality of death the conviction that God is the giver of life and not of death, will he eventually overcome the last great enemy, this is making Health certain.

All the ancient philosophers taught the deathless life, and broadly hinted at the coming time when man should not be a suffering weakling constantly in the throes of death; but reach perfection of both body and soul while on the earth plane. However, it remained for Jesus to demonstrate to mankind the possibility of so purifying and developing the physical being that it might even be taken up again after life had actually departed from it.

Just as Jesus lived the life that brought him the Sublime Realization, and the attainment of the sinless, diseaseless, and deathless life, so brought he man the promise and gave him the instruction which should gradually bring him from death in life, to Conscious Individuality and continued health. But man has lacked the faith that would induce him to live the deathless life, which would help him to reach the ultimate. One of the teachings, which, according to this claim, was given the master teacher by the Father, for the instruction of mankind, is this: "Whosoever shall eat of the bread that I give, shall have eternal life." The bread referred to, is wisdom; true under-standing of the laws of life! and the one 'who lives accordingly *shall have life unto eternity;* moreover, it shall be one of peace, of happiness, and of contentment.

These sublime philosophies—the Christic Interpretation of the "bread of life"—covered over by much rubbish during the centuries of creedism, the Humanitarians now place before the people. Whosoever is wiling to live according to these instructions shall find health and freedom from the miseries so prevalent among mankind at the present time. This is the divine purpose, the universal plan, for man—the attaiment of Conscious Individuality, the Realization of life without death. To support this infinite purpose, to re-establish faith in the divinity, is the mission of the New Commandment, and will make Health certain.

The doctrine of a life without death is based on the Divine Law, on the Sacred Scriptures, and the ancient philosophies as understood by all the great masters and initiates of the various ages. That the ultimate of man's destiny is eternal life and the consciousness of immortality, has eternally been the standard of all true Initiatory Rites of revealed religion; and the victory over death demonstrated by the Initiate Jesus, is for all who will meet the requirements of the Divine Law as he met them in actual experience.

Let no one be induced to believe, that by some miraculous display, man may through one great effort grasp great power; potential force is the culmination of soul development extending through a period of living and training; the conservation of energy, and harmonizing with both natural and divine law. There is a science of development for both body and mind, one that fully explains laws and methods, and points "the Way, the Truth, and the Life" underlying Conscious growth. To teach mankind these laws governing on both the physical and spiritual plane, is the purpose of the Humanitarians and of the Christic Interpretation.

In the very beginning must be broken the fetters of the age-old belief in the unconquerable universality, aye, even of the necessity, of sin, disease and failure; and there must be substituted in the minds and hearts of men the conviction that these undesirable visitants are not according to the divine purpose for man, but that, being created in the image of God, he is endowed with divine attributes and powers, which when developed and rightly employed, will enable him, ultimately, to overcome all his weakness, create success, and make Health certain.

Advancement in any line whatsoever, demands a beginning. With many into whose hands these pages fall, this has already been made. The fact that one accepts books or manuscripts of this nature, and carefully ponders thereon, is in itself proof of interest, of an awakening of mind to greater possibilities than heretofore known. Interest along this trend of thought, a desire for truth, and persistence in overcoming carnality and the supremacy of the lower nature, leads to life more abundantly. The tendency to indulge in negative destructive thought habits leads to death; this must be changed into aspiration for knowledge, for strength, and for success, eventually assuring health and happiness.

Man may be thoroughly convinced that life according to the Divine Plan is the only true and satisfactory state; yet it seems easier for him to follow the dictates of the carnal self; this is because his whole nature is negative; it will require a positive and persistent effort to arouse himself from such lethargy, into the action essential to living the Ideal established by the Infinite. The majority of mankind are still controlled by the desires of the personality, and living in harmony with the laws of sin, sickness, and death, rather than with the universal law governing life, and health, and success; often extreme sorrow, absolute failure, or excruciating suffering will arouse and induce them to the effort necessary in obtaining their freedom from the bondage.

Great changes are taking place; man is beginning to think; to search for the cause of conditions which enslave him. He is investigating the relation existing between cause and effect; he questions *why* such misery and suffering. He beholds the life as lived by mankind generally and associates the effect with the mode of living, and clearly recognizes something is lacking; gradually, reaching the conclusion, that, having tested the old way, lo, these many centuries, he will now try the new; for this cannot be worse than the former. As he casts aside the old and commences to live the life of faith attended by works corresponding thereto, results are gratifying, even more so than he had anticipated, or thought possible. Thus, not merely the one, nor yet the few, but the many are being awakened to the spirit of the new age. The old race belief in death is being replaced by the new in life and freedom; making Health certain.

It is not at all difficult to determine the reason for conditions when one understands the law of correspondence. This law exists between all things; between that which is the above and the below; between the universe and God; between the universe and man, and between man and God, his Creator. The body is of the earth, material. The soul is of the heaven, spiritual. Conditions depend on which power is in the ascendancy. If the body and its passions are in control the conditions of man's life tend toward disease and death. If the Soul is awakening and the Still Small Voice called Intuition, can be heard, then man's life and character will commence to exemplify, satisfactory correspondence with God and the universe, manifesting the fact of his being created in the divine image.

With rare exceptions, to the man of the present age, the soul is merely a weird something to believe in; of which there is no certain knowledge; no tangible evidence; while the body is visible, able to experience pain and pleasure. Consequently the body is a reality, and the soul at best but a fanciful theory. To these many citizens of the world, the body has a right to claim superior attention and this would not be so discouraging if the attention given it was of the right kind, but nearly all cater to the desires and appetites, cravings which, when indulged in to excess or contrary to wise guidance, lead to disease, weakness, failure, and death, and until the desires of the flesh have been made subservient to the wisdom of the soul they lead downward.

The aspirations of the soul are different both in immediate effect and in permanent results. The soul, being of God, in its longing and its inclinations, reached upwards; but, being unseen and hardly felt, man brushes aside the impulses and the intuitions of the spirit; with the result that the prototype of God in man has been lulled asleep; has been dormant and inactive, until its Voice can no longer be heard.

When the voice of the soul, the divine urge, becomes audible and is obeyed; then, step by step, it leads itself and its physical vehicle upwards until eventually Conscious Individuality is attained and life without death, is reached. Thus, man frees himself not only from disease and death, but likewise from all that is undesirable. In addition, besides casting aside the bonds of affliction, the soul, the spiritual counterpart of God, comes into harmony with the Father, and tastes of the Sublime Realization.

This life, in which the soul maintains supremacy over the body, is the one the greater teacher lived. He had faith in the instructions he had received from the philosophers under whom he studied; and, as he lived in harmony with the laws taught, he gradually attained the Divine Realization, until, finally, he had so perfected and refined the body that it was no longer the slave to sickness; obtained freedom from sorrow and misery; and was qualified to manifest ultimate victory over death and to come into the glory of God while in the flesh. According to the divine promise, all men may, if they will, live as did Jesus; and through faithful, persistent obedience to the Law, find it possible to obtain health, strength, success; reach Conscious Individuality, and *know* God.

Let none believe that a life thus indicated, whereby one may obtain victory over disease and failure, is not real or practical. The contrary is true, for the manly man is neither a parasite nor an unprofitable or undesirable member of society; he lives a life of service; engages in business, and fulfills the responsibilities that devolve on all men. He is faithful to the duties of home life and neighborhood interests, and is responsive to all worthy demands of society at large. Nor must it be thought that he who desires to realize the power of the Christ over death and the grave is to deny himself all pleasures and all recreation and all delights. Here, also, the contrary is true, he is entitled to all innocent and harmless pleasures, to recreation and all that is conducive to health, and in which normal human beings delight. The only check on pleasure of any description is the proviso that it be free from harm to himself and others.

Man is by nature a social being; of all creatures, he is the only one blessed with the smile and the laugh; this in itself clearly indicates that the festive instinct and the gift of smile and laughter were given him for a purpose. The more he encourages the wholesome spirit of merriment and amiability, the better for himself and all with whom he comes in contact. The life of those who have reached Conscious Individuality is not an aimless, insipid, unattractive existence; nothing that is truly good is denied him, whether it be for his profit or enjoyment. All is his if he will use it for a right and noble purpose whereby to benefit himself and others.

That man may reach the highest, he must perfect both

body and soul. Were he to develop body alone, free it from sickness and weakness, he would be no more than a superb animal. To be an attuned instrument, the Inner Man, the Soul, must be awakened, and through this come into direct personal touch and communion with the Father and the invisible forces and potencies, hence making health, strength and success certain, and establishing communion with the higher realm.

How may communion be established? Through fellowship with the Father, obtained much easier than man generally would believe. It results in a holy alliance with the Creator, which raises man gradually to the very highest. The best method is through heart prayer in the silence and by means of Sacred Mantrams definitely formed with a purpose in view and strictly adhered to; held in the heart to the exclusion of all else; these are of no benefit if the lips frame words totally contrary to the acts of life.

Communion is not immediately accomplishable. The child just commencing to talk is not understood by the parents, any more than it can comprehend all the parents say, however plainly they may speak. Nevertheless, every heart prayer, however imperfect at first, is understood by the Father; while we, on our part, will gradually grasp the meaning of the divine language, if we remain faithful and heartwhole, and soon hear the heavenly music. Thus in time, does man attain perfection of body; freedom from sin, sickness, and failure; and finally, the consummation of the divine plan—Conscious Individuality.

Truth Means Freedom

Learn to know the truth, then live according to the truth. Believe actively that the life of the Christ (Nature and God) is good; that man is *not* born to suffering and disease; nor need he be a creature of pain and misery if he is willing to comply with the natural and divine law. Let each one live in harmony with the truth that man is made in the image of the Creator, God; casting aside forever the thought that he must suffer and "surely die." Instill in its place the conviction that you are a child of the Father, who has given you all power; that sin and sickness are not for you, but instead, more and continually more of life are yours, ending in Conscious Individuality or Immortality.

Chapter Five

The Destructive Life Ends in Death

Scientists maintain that the entire vegetable, animal, and human kingdoms are governed by the Law of evolution. In so far as the ordinary life of these realms is concerned, the theory of evolution is correct; but the evolutionist, as a rule, fails to take into consideration one important item, namely: the fact that man, having free will (no matter how obtained, or by whom conferred), has the privilege of working in harmony with the laws of nature; and, when he awakens to this truth, he is no longer bound by the iron rule of evolution, nor his growth retarded by it; but through co-operation may quickly step beyond it. To work in harmony with evolution, yet transcend its pace, man must understand the greater law; that of *interior* Development; and by using all his forces, be enabled to accomplish in one lifetime as much as the evolutionary process could in thousands of years.

When man awakens from the deadening influence of the carnal self, and commences to recognize his inherent powers, he sets into motion new laws (or rather, laws which were heretofore not utilized by him); and, instead of remaining a pawn in the grasp of the evolutionary law, he achieves the mastery, works in harmony with, yet superior to, the law of evolution; thus life becomes an *unfoldment*, a growth, in which he himself has *conscious* share; whereas, without this voluntary co-operation, he is retarded, or pushed forward, merely because it must needs be so; for the law forces him to slowly move, whether he will or not.

The power of *interior* Unfoldment is not new to men; it is neither an invention or a discovery of modern times, nor is it the product of a fanatical or fanciful imagination. It is a decree that was known to the Masters of all ages; the Ancient Egyptians made use of it in the training of their priests. Every Neophyte in the ancient Priesthood developed and was trained under this divine edict. Egyptian priests who understood perfectly the Laws governing *interior* Development and Unfoldment, as well as those of Evolution, taught and trained Jesus unto Mastership; this is admitted by Sacred Scripture.

The evolutionary potency may accomplish as much as will Conscious Development; but the fact remains that, by following the method of Conscious Development, man may attain in one short lifetime what nature and her laws, working alone, would require thousands of years, aye, possibly cycles.

This fact is frequently illustrated in the animal kingdom, which, unless man interferes, is governed by the law of evolution. Any animal would serve as an illustration; but, to be specific, we choose the common hen. Given her freedom and allowed to mate as she pleases, there would be practically no improvement in her progeny, even within a period of many years; but, one having a full understanding of the rules governing correct mating and improvement of the specie, taking charge of her, breeding and feeding her properly, can produce super-hens within a period of five years. Instead of the continuation of mongrel stock, both in respect to type and the production of eggs, the standard, or near standard of type, can be obtained, as also the maximum of egg production. This merely implies that, in the improvement of the specie, man no longer must blindly depend on evolutionary forces, but working in harmony with them *and* employing the higher law—that of Universal development, may secure almost unbelievable results.

Identically the same laws apply to man. If left to nature and the forces of evolution, it is possible that he may, in the period of aeons and cycles, become a Soul Illuminated being, but, if he awakens to the possibilities of his destiny, working in harmony with the universal laws of progress, making *Conscious* and *voluntary* use of the Laws governing Interior development and unfoldment, he can in a comparatively short time, attain Conscious Individuality.

Free choice is the privilege of man. This is the age of enlightenment; wherein truth is being apportioned among mankind. The infinite possibilities of man's nature are now clearly pointed out; he is being taught that instead of remaining slavishly "a worm of the dust," he has within himself the germ of Godhood, and all that is required of him is to live in harmony with natural and divine laws. If he is willing to do this faithfully and conscientiously, he soon will be on the way to power and success; making Health certain.

Even those who consider Jesus merely as a great philosopher, and not in very truth the Son of God, would do well to heed his instructions governing the Law of Conscious Development and Interior Unfoldment. While those who think slightingly of the Sacred Scriptures might profit by adopting for their standard the doctrine that culminates in victory over death and the grave.

"O death, where is thy sting, O grave, where is thy victory?" This expression is not a mere literary phrase, nor is it a fanciful theory; rather, it expresses ultimate truth to those who understand that death is not merely the process of the spirit leaving the body, but includes the sinful, sorrowful, painful and unsuccessful existence of the multitudes. After the animal nature has been mastered, the soul will arise free and in glory from the experiences of a living death; then it is apprehended as indeed true that in death there is no sting.

The exclamation, "O death, where is thy sting, O grave, where is thy victory?" would have very little value in itself to mankind had it not time and again been demonstrated by the Illuminated that death has no terror for those who obey the laws governing Development and Interior Unfoldment. In his time, the Master Jesus revealed that the fruits of living in harmony with the rules of Development are mastery over sin, sickness, and failure; clearly indicating that as he had been able to overcome these enemies of the race, so might all men willing to be governed by these laws, thus making Health certain.

The true life of man is one of *Interior* Development,—growth from one degree of being to another, a continuous unfoldment which leads from carnality and selfishness upward to the plane of Godhood and Sonship. Startling as this doctrine may appear to many, yet, nowhere in the Scripture, nor in the philosophies, is there a single statement contradictory to this principle; but everywhere, on every hand, search where we may, is voluminous evidence of its truth.

True, there is on record this saying: "Man that is born of woman is of few days and full of trouble." Taken in its literal interpretation, this statement contradicts the *doctrine of life, joy, and immortality we annunciate*. However, the New Commandment in its Christic Interpretation, fearlessly maintains that when man has awakened from his carnal nature by accepting the Divine Law as his standard, and living in obedience with the Law of *Interior Unfoldment*, he *no longer is to be considered as* "man that is born of woman," but truly as "man that is born of God." In the process of development, his carnal nature, aye, even his material body, has been changed into the finer, more electric, being; therefore has been "born again," born of God, and is more or less, according to the degree of unfoldment, free from the bondage that previously bound him. "Man that is born of woman" is full of trouble; admittedly true, but man that is born of God is no longer under such serfdom, because conditions previously thought of as sorrows he has learned to consider as valuable experiences of life; *stepping stones to a greater and a higher existence.* As man born of God, he is heir to Life, Light, and Immortality.

Through such principles do we, the Humanitarians, lead our disciples away from the grave and realms of weakness; from the belief that our Creator is a God of death, unto the Sphere of Life and Love, Success and Happiness; making Health certain.

The path of death, the carnal life, leads only to death; this is a self-evident truth; and in this realm, is man truly born of woman, of a few days, and full of sorrow. All this, however, the awakened man quickly changes; he casts off the shackles of disease, weakness, and failure,—the living death; likewise of ignorance and fear; and, standing boldly before God, the Giver of life, demands the heritage that is rightly his,—that of Life, of Light, and of Love, ending in Immortality.

The path of death leads to death; but there is a higher, a greater life—one that is free from the passions that destroy; that gradually liberates itself from the destroyers,—anger and jealousy, malice and resentment; establishing in their place love and forgiveness.

One of the most important tasks for man to undertake on entering the rejuvenating life is to free himself from the destructive evil, termed the "red Light of Death"—anger. Significant, indeed is the maxim of the ancient philosophers, "Him whom the gods would destroy they first make mad," nor is it other than a literal statement of truth. Anger quickly fills the entire being—body, mind, and soul, with poison; often bringing death in its path. He who gives way to anger loses the sense of righteous judgment; and, while in the passion, committing deeds he would not while in his rational mind. So great is the virus generated by this passion that it has often caused death outright through apoplexy; moreover, a fit of anger has been known to poison the milk of a nursing mother to a degree sufficiently virulent to cause the death of her suckling babe. The first step, therefore, in the overcoming of sickness, weakness, and failure, is to gain mastery over the self; the overcoming of a hasty temper; the foundation whereon rest all other destructive passions.

That health of body, tranquility of mind, and sublimity of soul be assured, this passion must be transmuted. Left unrestrained, it tends towards disease, unhappiness, failure; eventually, death itself. Furthermore, when man overcomes this pernicious weakness, he will be able, through the power acquired, to gain the victory over the lesser negative emotions; as a result, making Health certain.

There are other degrading passions to which carnal man is prone to fall victim. Among these are jealousy, envy, fault-finding, and harsh criticism of the failings, real or fancied, of our fellow beings. All these, destructive in the extreme, have been called the "green passions;" because they create a poison green in color, and give an aura of a green tinge, the color of destructiveness.

The tendency to anger and impatience is well-nigh universal; almost all mankind is in its grip. Ofttimes it finds lodging in those who are nearing the goal of a Regenerative life. One on the path to Life and Rejuvenation, although having overcome the passion of anger or an obstinate temper, may be in the grip of that other insiduous destroyer: the sin of faultfinding. He who has not mastered this tendency to find fault with the habits and the life of others, has still a deadly enemy within to combat.

This does not infer that the teacher, or the guide, of a seeker should not inform him of inherent weaknesses, and indicate the best method of overcoming them; such is his duty; but, if one is not the instructor of others nor in authority over them, he has not the right or privilege to criticise their actions. He has a greater and more important work right at home,—the task of mastering the passions that induce discomfort, disease, and failure in himself.

To give rein to any of the destructive passions, proves that we are, for the time being following the path of death; and, while we may be earnestly groping for the light of life, we are, nevertheless, in the grasp of the grim reaper.

Jesus, like other philosophers before him, came as a teacher of the truth; but he did more than this; *he lived the truth, demonstrated the fact that his doctrine would lead one from death to life.* Moreover, he explicitly emphasized that the life he taught could be lived by all who truly desired to do so; he also proved the superiority of the Christos over sin, sickness and the grave, making Health certain.

There are two media by which man may demonstrate the Rejuvenating process. One is by purifying and refining the body to such a degree that the soul may lay it down in death, leave it temporary, then return and take it up again. The other is to demonstrate health, strength, success, and happiness, in the material existence. The body may be so refined and regenerated that its existence blends, and becomes as one, with the soul.

Jesus could not demonstrate the two methods at the same time; he could only manifest in one or the other; and, as mankind was in ignorance concerning the practical features of immortality, he chose the lesser first; thereby he proved that the Soul lives after the death of the body and may claim the body as an instrument of communication on the human plane even after the Great Transition.

The seeker must also remember that He had long been prophesied as one who was to come who would be able to give up the life of the body, and, after a certain period of time, sufficiently lengthy to prove the body lifeless, take it up again; he fulfilled this prophecy.

Jesus in turn prophesied a time would surely come when man could do even greater things than he; when man would demonstrate sin, sickness and failure as unnecessary. That time is *now;* man may so live in harmony with natural and divine law that the body itself, together with the soul, may be rejuvenated and regenerated, making Health certain.

We, as Humanitarians, in the New Commandment, inculcate these truths and the way to fulfillment. We fearlessly maintain that, if the instructions we formulate are faithfully obeyed, the sayings of Jesus will be fulfilled, and man will eventually overcome the great enemies to happiness. Let it be emphasized, however, that such power as this cannot be developed in a short time or by any crude, haphazard method; nor is any claim made that all mankind may attain the potential energy necessary to manifest health, strength and success, unless weaknesses are overcome and the truths taught, accepted. The majestic oak is not grown in a day and a night, neither is *Interior* Unfoldment a hot house growth. Let it be emblazoned in *fire* that the carnal life is destructive; while exalted thought, obedience to natural and divine law, and simplicity, in life's habits, make Health certain.

Chapter Six

Truth Is Without Compassion

Historical research reveals that every age has had its philosophers, teachers, and saviors, who, becoming converts to truth, and denying the self until they reached enlightenment, gave the people of that age much of the wisdom they had gained; knowledge not learned from books, or in the study of age old manuscripts, but obtained from experience through *actual living.*

Likewise, history records the mistakes of many men and women attracted to these philosophers and sages, under the false impression that they might attain mastery for themselves without living the Life that gained the precious jewels for those who were teaching. These foolish ones longed to come into possession of the knowledge and power possessed by the philosophers and masters; but were unwilling to deny themselves as these had done; deluded with the mistaken idea that wisdom might be attained, and power obtained, while continuing the life of sin and death. In their worldly carnal mindedness, they thought to lay hold of truth, wisdom, understanding, and all that is desirable, by simply believing, or through a formal confession of faith. They utterly failed to recognize that man cannot obtain any tangible possession legitimately, no matter what its nature, unless he is ready and willing to either work for, or deny himself in some manner, thereby honestly earning it.

Truth, in the beginning, undoubtedly appears a hard master. Truth commands: Thus shalt thou if thou wouldst receive. And, unless we are willing to abide by the dictates of Truth and Wisdom we will not obtain—*we will be unable to receive.* Wisdom and power demand their own price; only he who is willing to pay the fee, *always demanded in advance,* will be given, or may become.

Indeed, were it possible to gain powers through might, rather than right, they would turn to bitter fruit, for "thou shalt not take the kingdom of heaven by storm," nor yet as "a thief in the night." No man can long retain that which he obtained illegitimately. Thus is it recorded that many lived who have knelt at the feet of some great master or teacher; listening attentively to his instructions, and believing foolishly they were able to employ, for their personal benefit, the power and wisdom indicated, though making no attempt to live, thereby accumulating the forces which would create energy and bring enlightenment. These gained a superficial comprehension of the Master's words, and undertook to apply them to life's needs, only to find the power evade their grasp—they had not earned possession.

Truth belongs only to him who earns it through the price paid in *becoming;* it is not an acquisition gained by mere intellectual effort. Knowledge is the result of *becoming,* of *being,* of *living in harmony with the laws of wisdom.* It is the acme of *Interior* Unfoldment; the natural result of spiritual growth.

The true teacher fully comprehends that truth cannot be attained in any superficial way; and when he places before the people a choice—either to *live* and possess, or not to obtain— they turn away from him and seek elsewhere; still believing there is some easy path to power; but, alas, they find when life is spent they were in quest of that which has no existence; the Law is absolute, and clearly states; "Thus must thou *do,* if thou wouldst possess."

In the time of Jesus, for instance, it was no different in many respects, from previous centuries. When he attempted to teach the multitudes that sin, sickness, and death were unnecessary the people would give no credence to his words. Even many

of the disciples who had witnessed the wonderful works per-
formed by him, turned and said: "This is a hard saying, Who
can hear it?"

And why? Merely because they were neither ready nor willing to accept great truths. The race belief could not even accept
the possibility of Immortality of the Soul, or the life beyond the
grave, how much less was it possible for them to accept a doctrine that advocated the life of health, strength, happiness, and
success? Thus, the people turned away from Jesus, and his life-
giving instructions; and, through this lack of faith, this turning
aside from the path of life, this refusal to accept the truth when
offered, because it seemed hard and *demanded something of them,*
missed not only the blessing of Conscious Individuality, but likewise, Health, strength and power.

It is not different in the present age. Many come to us for
instruction who believe in the Immortality of the Soul; but are
unwilling to apply the teachings to their individual needs. They
will not live in obedience to the law of Interior Development,
hence experiencing the proof of the Soul's reality; they demand
some outward manifestation of power, aye, even a vision of the
Heavenly Host, before they will be willing to obey.

These forget the fact that the laborer is not paid before he
has served; that God forces no man to either believe or accept, or to live, but gives to all men free-will to do as they
please, attaching, at the same time, the penalty which applies to
disobedience, or the reward for living in harmony with both
natural and divine law. He offers man the privilege of obtaining
the knowledge which would gain for him the boon of Health,
strength, power, happiness and success; yet it is equally true
He gives to no one that which is not honestly earned; neither
does He degrade His power by showing man signs and wonders

inducing him to accept the doctrine which brings *life*. On the contrary, He plainly voices, through the Philosophers and teachers, the credo that man shall *not* seek for signs and wonders, but *live and thereby manifest*.

Time and again did Jesus, as also many other leaders before his time, attempt to teach the multitude that sin, sickness, and failure are not necessary, but the result of disobedience; in the end, he found few who would accept the hard saying. These superficial seekers merely left him and followed pseudo-philosophers who showed them what purported to be an easier way to the life of power. Even those continually with the Master found it difficult to accept the doctrine of immortality, and Conscious Individuality, the. Path to Health and happiness; and impossible of comprehension when he taught that he was to lay down his body and take it up again, so demonstrating there is no death, only a change.

Lastly, when the many had forsaken him, he sought to teach the great truth to his disciples by saying, "Verily, verily, I say unto you, if a man keep my word, he shall not see death." This, indeed, was a hard saying; one the few would then accept, and to which many are callous today; this is why sin, sickness, weakness, and failure, abound throughout the world.

The expectation to obtain and possess health, strength, power and happiness, through mere belief while continuing in a life of carnality and selfishness, dwells in the heart of many, and the leaders who flount before the people such a destructive doctrine are well supported and largely followed, but Jesus never offered mankind such a false standard. A credence which permits one to live the life of sin, ignorance, and error, with the expectancy of health, strength, and immortality, is founded on illusion. Only that deserves the name of true faith which stimulates activity and an endeavor to realize and manifest the fruits of it; faith is essential, but living in harmony with it is absolutely necessary if lasting results are to follow. "Keep the word" is the command, then will one obtain the benefits of the promise; which are: freedom from disease, from failure, from weakness; ultimately Conscious Individuality and eternal advancement. Much, however, remains to be accomplished and realized in man's experience before this ideal may be generally sought; the overcoming of the race belief in the necessity of sickness and failure, alone will be a wonderful achievement.

In its highest phase, *life is an unfoldment*. To begin with, man is of the earth, earthly; and, from the material, draws his strength. Man may be likened to the rose tree, of which he is a prototype. The roots of the tree are in the earth, from the soil it receives strength and vitality; gradually, in *obedience to the natural law*, it leans toward the sun; as it lives and grows into a specimen of great strength and symmetry, the time arrives for a manifestation of its inherent beauty; then the bud appears, soon the full blown rose; it has attained its highest degree of perfection; its blossoms symbolize immortality, even though the roots of the tree are deep in the material.

Man should follow the example of the rose tree. Though of the earth, and from which he must draw sustenance, he should obey the divine law; gradually developing within himself the Conscious Soul, symbolic of the beautiful rose, and, ultimately, the Soul will reach enlightenment, or Illumination, then will he have obtained Health, strength, success, and happiness; Immortality is assured him. There is but one difference between man and the rose tree. Man has free will and can disobey God's law, while the tree has no choice, it must obey; consequently, almost every rose tree will reach its highest attainment and produce roses—its Illumination, while in the human kingdom but few achieve, because many disobey.

This is the Law. It is a hard saying. Few are willing to believe it. It is a truth nevertheless; one that all may accept and thereby reap the reward for living in harmony with it. *All constructive laws are hard,* in the sense that they are inflexible and offer no premium for their acceptation. Man seems, since his birth upon earth, to have been, and to remain, bargain-counter mad. He is eternally looking for special offers, for an easy way to live, or to gain possession of that which he desires. Only the few are willing to pay, to the last pence, for everything they seek; these few become the Immortals; they are on the Path to Conscious Individuality; to Health, strength, and power.

What is the argument of the multitudes against the doctrine of Immortality of the whole man?

There has been little change since the first century: "Abraham is dead. So are the prophets. Is any man greater than these?"

Because men have died and continue to die, because men are weak and diseased, in misery and failures, is this a proof it must ever be so? Once upon a time it was necessary to carry freight by means of horses and cart, there being no other method of transportation, then boats and rails were invented and all was changed; but before goods were actually conveyed by these modern methods, only the few would believe the prophecy it should be otherwise in the good time coming; and when this was fulfilled, the many considered it as the work of the devil; so difficult is it for man to accept the new, though infinitely better way. Knowing this, we cannot wonder it is hard for man to believe in anything but death, sickness, weakness, and failure;

the fetters of the age-long race belief are as yet too strong for him.

The multitudes demand signs and wonders; they will not accept the truth unless demonstrated in some miraculous manner; even then when one, freed from the race belief in the necessity of sickness, weakness, and death, commences to live in harmony with truth, and demonstrates its efficacy, the many wag their wise heads and exclaim: "Wait and see, shortly he will be as others are." It may be centuries before the doctrine inculcated by the Philosophers of the past, and now again in the New Commandment, will be largely approved. In the meantime, those who will cast aside prejudice or through suffering be forced to accept, and live, will make Health certain.

In the beginning, truth, apparently, is hard; and to follow its dictates, difficult; but, when man does finally harmonize his life with the law and commence to manifest the results, he will find himself well repaid and happy for having made the effort. Truth is an exacting mistress, but she offers ample returns for her exactitude, all of the true life is governed by the same law.

"Keep my word, and ye shall never see death." This is not merely the inculcation of a doctrine as outlined by Jesus; it is the Divine Command; has always been, will always be. *Live the life,* is a plain, literal translation. Live in harmony with the Law, then you will reap the benefits, the rewards; this is making Health certain, Immortality absolute.

We wish to so emphatically declare that none may mistake, that just as faith of itself is not sufficient, so is right living not the whole of the law. Were correct living alone sufficient, then the animal of the field, existing in harmony with nature would have continuous, immortal life. Faith and right living, and a *conscious effort to attain,* is the whole (holy) law. Neither one nor the other is complete in itself, though living makes the probable possible. Belief, or faith, so charges, magnetizes, or aetherizes the soul, that it, having gradually become Conscious of God, raises the vibrations of the entire body, to the Immortal plane.

The Humanitarians, through the New Commandment, teach that neither faith nor obedience to the law, alone is sufficient whereby to reach the highest goal of achievement, but that understanding of truth and faith in the truth, together with living in harmony with the wisdom possessed, are essential to reach Conscious Individuality and know the Father, making Health and Immortality certain.

Unlike other doctrines respecting immortality, we do not teach that man, in attaining the final goal, loses his individuality and once again becomes a part of the Godhead. We maintain, on the contrary, definitely and emphatically, that man becomes an absolute, conscious individuality, free from all that is carnal and gross, and knowing the Father, a co-worker with Him.

Nor is this doctrine of the immortality of the whole (holy) man without example. There have been, unless you deny Biblical authority, those who walked with God—that is, had faith in God and His promises and lived accordingly—who were taken up body and soul, into the high heavens, and *know* God Of these are Enoch, Elijah and Moses, the Lawgiver. These believed as the ancient Priests taught; they had faith in God, in His promises, through the faith and the personification of it in works, they were able to fulfill the covenant made between God and man.

All men may do likewise. To do so it is essential for the hard, (inflexible) truth to be believed, for the hard (absolute) sayings to be accepted. It is imperative man shall not run after signs and wonders, after manifestations, a la Ouija board, and pseudo-mediums supposed to transact business between man and spirits. It is necessary for man to be the actor, rather than the one acted upon as a machine is manipulated by the master intellect; that he *become* the Son of God through faith and works; living in harmony with the law, thereby attaining Conscious Immortality.

God's law is eternal, unchangeable, and non-transferable; always remember this. It is the Divine Law of which Nature's law is a part. It is absolute *non-failing.* Though we think of it as a hard truth (because it demands obedience), nevertheless, when we become willing instruments, we find it is not a difficult life to live. It may seem hard in the beginning, but we soon learn no good thing is forbidden us.

To repeat: The perfect life is faith accompanied by works. But we must ever be on our guard lest our faith become centered in personalities, who as best have weaknesses; and, if we are not watchful, we will judge them by this weakness and forget their strength and their services to mankind. The perfect life is one of service; it is not built on mere belief, a negative condition of existence, but, first and last, a courageous struggle to *become.* Finally, life is a *growth,* an *unfoldment—* commencing on the material plane, gradually reaching toward the state of consciousness wherein we realize that the carnal activity is not true being, finally leading to the plane of existence wherein the individuality merges into, and identifies itself with, the Divine; nevertheless retaining its individual consciousness and identity; thus man becomes an immortal, deathless being, making Health and success, happiness and peace, certain. Such is the destiny of man.

The Practical Life

Let none believe that a life thus indicated, whereby one may obtain victory over disease and failure, is not real or practical. The contrary is true, for the manly man is neither a parasite nor an unprofitable or undesirable member of society; he lives a life of service; engages in business, and fulfills the responsibilities that devolve on all men. He is faithful to the duties of home life and neighborhood interests, and is responsive to all worthy demands of society at large. Nor must it be thought that he who desires to realize the power of the Christ over death and the grave is to deny himself all pleasures and all recreation and all delights. Here, also, the contrary is true, he is entitled to all innocent and harmless pleasures, to recreation and all that is conducive to health, and in which normal human beings delight. The only check on pleasure of any description is the proviso that it be free from harm to himself and others.

Chapter Seven

To Glorify God Is Man's Duty

Did God create man and His other creatures with the intention of destroying them, or that they should live and work to His glory? Does man, though a finite being, create that he may have the pleasure of demolishing the products of his labor, or that it shall be of benefit and welfare to himself and the race?

Question ourselves as we may, we come to the one only conclusion; namely, that in creating we do it because it seems necessary, either for our own benefit or for that of others. Moreover having given existence, we do not consider it well to destroy; though, at times, as our knowledge increases, we may deem it best to change or improve our handiwork. If finite man in his efforts is prompted by altruistic motives, must we not conclude that God, being infinite and having created all that exists, has neither the desire to destroy his workmanship nor to make any change except such as come through normal, natural growth harmonizing with His laws? If this is admitted as true, we must conclude that it is not the divine plan or purpose for the soul of man to be destroyed, nor that the body should be continually ill, weak, and unfit for the labors assigned him by the Father of all creation.

Why, then, is the body of man subject to sickness and degeneration, ending in senility and decay?

There is but one rational answer. Man, through disobedience to the divine command to become like God, induces conditions making it impossible for the body to be healthy and strong, fit to meet all emergencies; therefore, man himself, and not his Creator, is responsible for the decay of the body and the mortality of the Soul. If this reasoning is correct, and who can question it, we come to the only possible conclusion—that is, the body of man was created, not to be weak and sickly; a burden, often a disgrace, but to glorify God through its strength and perfection; nor was the soul destined by the divine plan to eternal torment, but as a fitting representation of the Father.

Making our statements positive: Man is created in the image of the Creator, endowed with His attributes and faculties. It is the divine purpose that he shall develop his inherent potentialities in obedience to the Divine law; by living the constructive life becoming like the Father, and making of his body a pure, holy, and fitting temple for the living God.

Thus it is to glorify God—so to live that the soul may reflect the Divine Image through a life of humble service; that the body may become a temple wherein God may take up his permanent abode. This is the duty of man; the end and the aim of life. Moreover, to glorify God results in happiness, peace, contentment, strength, and success. When man finally comprehends this principle and harmonizes his little world with the divine standard set for him, then will life on earth become what it should be and as God had intended. This is the culmination, the ultimate goal, of glorifying God—to attain Conscious Individuality, inheritance of Immortality.

Nor is this doctrine in any way contradictory to the principles thus far advocated. It has long been taught that man may so regulate his life as to attain Rejuvenation of his being, or Illumination of the Soul—the consciousness of God, while in the flesh. This achievement is the result of a long-continued process that extends, in some instances, through many lives on earth;

at the experience called death, the soul, having failed in its labors, passes on to the soul realm to remain for a time, then being granted the privilege of returning to earth there completing its labors. This is termed the Law of Reincarnation, and governs all who have disobeyed God's command to "believe and *live* in me." These principles are by no means contradictory to the doctrine of immortality; they are stepping stones along the way, which lead to the higher, fuller life of the whole man; they are subordinate, yet in harmony with, the tenet of Conscious Individuality.

The doctrine of complete immortality maintains that the soul of man may find its heaven, its millenium, here on earth without going forth and returning. The ideal of working for a distant heaven, hoping to attain peace and happiness in the far-off future is no longer attractive to mankind. To look forward to a state of being in the Beyond, or in time to come, which the soul of man will attain after death and there enjoy, ceases to satisfy. Men desire to gain the knowledge, the wisdom, and the power that shall enable them to overcome ignorance, sin, disease, and weakness, here and now. They seek to become victorious coming to a realization that they are on the Path to mastery. They must be helped to a comprehension that now is a part of the Hereafter, a link in the chain of Eternity, and that today determines the status of tomorrow.

Men at last comprehend that disease is the result of ignorance, error, an wrongdoing; that illness is the penalty for disobedience, of living contrary to the laws governing health. It is becoming more and more a prevalent idea that life in the soul realm, in the Great Beyond, is merely a continuation of the present life. As we are now, so shall we be. The passions that bind the body now will hold the soul where there is no body.

The habits that enchain and enslave on the earth plane will bind and hamper in the soul realm. These constructive ideas are being daily deeply ingrained in the race consciousness. That the present determines the future is even now a race conviction; and that ignorance, error, sin, disease, failure, and even death, are conditions to be overcome, not granted passive resignation, is gradually becoming a race belief.

The race consciousness has too long been content with a religion that has unduly emphasized helpless submission to what was believed divine providence, a passive resignation to a so-called higher will; blind surrender to an unknown ruling power. The tide has at last turned; such teaching no longer gives comfort; the tendrils and the "feelers" of the race consciousness are gradually turning toward the light and are reaching out for a positive, active, virile religion. The multitudes are seeking light and understanding; a truth that will safely guide them. They are weary of being admonished to be submissive and resigned; of allowing themselves to be the plaything of unseen forces. They hunger for wisdom and the power that will enable them to become active creative agents, unconsciously feeling this would be the path to success and power.

On all sides we see evidence of ignorance, sin, disease, suffering, sorrow, and a death that knows no awakening. Under mysterious and unaccountable "ministrations of providence," man has known no better philosophy than to bow in submission, and to "bide a wee, and dinna fret." He now demands, *why?* He seeks the cause of "painful ministrations of providence"; and having discovered the root of the trouble he attempts removing it, preventing future like experiences. Hitherto, he has tried to glorify God by a negative, blind, inert meekness; now he longs to glorify God by conscious, deliberate, definite, painstaking effort to fulfill the Divine Purpose and to realize the Infinite plan. Heretofore, he thought to glorify God by saying, "Nevertheless, not my will, but thine be done." Now he stands upright as man should and sends forth the challenge: "I *will* that thy Will be done through me. I *will* to become an active instrument in thy hands. I put forth conscious, deliberate effort to direct the inherent potencies into channels of useful service."

The many have been foolishly exclaiming: "We want to believe; but you must show us some manifestation enabling us to have faith." The day is well-nigh at hand when the demand for outer demonstration of truth will be changed into the determination, "I will live the life leading to an *inner* realization of truth."

It is not reasonable to expect the doctrine of full and complete immortality to be accepted immediately and by great numbers. The blotting out of the old race belief and the establishment of a new and higher consciousness is at best a slow, gradual process; nor is it necessary to look at the ultimate in order to accept the higher truths. One may not desire bodily immortality, nor be attracted to the thought of heaven on earth, but where is there one in the vast multitude that does not desire freedom from disease and suffering, weakness and failure; who does not long for the severing of the bonds binding them to ignorance, error, sin, and sorrow? To seek this knowledge, and to accept the truth that leads to such enlightenment is an important step toward breaking down the long-standing race beliefs and establishing in the consciousness higher and purer motives, this will make Health certain.

A sincere aspiration for freedom from untoward conditions, great suffering, or deep sorrow, will induce one to accept the truth, and to live the life which leads away from these undesirable possessions. Living in harmony with the truth necessitates obedience to the Divine Law and eventually ends in Conscious Individuality. To believe the truth respecting the cause of that which is weakening and degrading, and to live in such manner as will free us, places us in harmony, and enables us to co-operate with, the law that advances us to the highest goal, even though we may not be conscious of striving for so great a prize.

The Law *is;* it includes and embraces all that is; the lesser is no less and no more than the beginning of the greater. As above, so below; as below, so above. As the lesser, so the greater. To accept the lesser and strive to achieve it, clears the way for the greater. Thus, step by step, degree by degree, the old race belief declines, and the new consciousness seeks higher planes; purer motives, and loftier ideals; until, eventually, belief in complete immortality, the possibility of Conscious Individuality and freedom from sickness and weakness, failure and sorrow, is becoming the universal faith.

What will be the result of obedience to the Law, both natural and divine?

Ultimately a perfect body; a creative, virile mind; these working in harmony, produce the perfect soul, the Christos, the consciousness of Oneness with the Supreme Creator.

Some object to the appellation "Christ," pleading in justification that the world has had enough of the Christ idea; demanding something more advanced. Such do not understand there can be nothing greater than the Christ principle. Another name might be substituted to designate it, yet the power this Principle represents, ever remains a mighty reality; the most potent factor known to man. Man may call himself the reincarnation of an ancient god of even a new incarnation direct from the Godhead, yet the eternal element in his being is ever the same; apply whatever name we please to it. No man has yet lived to the full the instructions formulated by Jesus; therefore the world can cite no perfect example of such a life; and the claim often made that they have lost their power is to illustrate gross ignorance in respect to the truth contained in them, and indicates superficial knowledge. The Christic teachings in their mystical sense have never been really understood and believed, much less lived and demonstrated.

To know the Christ is to have attained Regeneration of being, or, term it, Illumination of Soul; it means that, through a system of living in obedience to natural and divine law, man attains the Consciousness of Christ in the Father. To have achieved such a degree of growth is to have freed the self from the grosser passions, to have made the body whole (holy). Moreover, it is the state of consciousness in which the soul can say as did Jesus, "I am the resurrection and the life." Then does man cease to merely exist; he lives on a higher plane than heretofore. Born not only of his mother, in the pain and sorrow of the flesh, but born of God into the realm of Spiritual Consciousness, he can truly exclaim: "I am the resurrection and the life." The Divine Spark of the soul within him has been nurtured and fed until it has become a brilliant Flame of Love, Wisdom and Power; he has beheld the Fire, part of the heavenly vision; he *knows* that he lives and shall not surely die.

All this is the inheritance of him who believes the truth and lives in harmony with it. Even though man still clings to the race belief in the necessity of death, Illumination of the Soul or Spiritual being, and the Consciousness of Immortality may be awakened; this allies one with the Father, Creator of all—"Him in whom we live and move and have our being."

It was the Christic Principle in Jesus that gave utterance to the prophecy, "He that liveth and believeth in me shall never die." This saying gave no foundation for centering our faith in a personality; no basis for the doctrine that belief in a historic character of Jesus, or even that he was the Son of God in itself insures salvation, the inheritance of a heavenly mansion. He that liveth and believeth in the Christ—shall never die. Such is the promise. If we live and serve humanity as did Jesus, and other teachers before him, not merely in slavish imitation of these sublime leaders, but in obedience to the Divine Law which rules life and cnters in our consciousness, then we shall find life eternal; and freed from erroneous race belief, we shall not know death.

Man has been following the letter and not the spirit of the Law; he has placed his faith in the personality of Jesus. Some, admittedly, believe in the existence of the Soul, but not in the Christ; but this in itself, though of some value, avails little. To have trust in the personality of some historic character, no matter how sublime such may have been, is not sufficient for salvation; but to have faith in the Law by, and through which, that particular personality was enabled to reach Conscious Individuality and Immortality, and to *obey* that Law, is the Divine command.

This is to glorify God—to establish faith in a Divine Principle—to live it. This is the significance of the mission of the teacher, Jesus. In his personality and in his individuality was exemplified the *law*, that, through this, it might be accepted by others as a guide; it remains for others to obey it as he did, thereby manifesting and reaping the fruits of such obedience.

The soul of man, which is the nucleus of all power, is as

deathless as He who created it. God cannot manifest without a medium; man is *that* medium. Likewise, the soul cannot reveal itself unless it has a medium; the body of man is the vehicle through which it portrays its character. It is just as reasonable to claim that God, whereby to save Himself, must destroy man through which he manifests, as to claim that man must, in order to save the soul, destroy the body or allow it to degenerate.

God does not destroy. Man, through disobedience to the Law, may annihilate himself entirely. Death of the body is not a necessity; but man, through ignorance. may induce its destruction; though nothing is gained through death, nor does the soul become either more sublime or advanced. On the contrary, the more man purifies the body and perfects it through obedience to law and order, the greater is his glorification of God; likewise, in proportion as he purifies and exalts the body, in that degree is the soul made purer and more sublime, until after the Baptism of Fire, it reaches to heaven and comes into conscious relationship with the Creator, *even though it yet remains in the body*.

It is the purpose and duty of man to so live as to glorify God and thus bring the Soul to Consciousness. In doing this, he is actually living the Christic life, and this continued, ultimately results in complete and full immortality and places him on the plane of consciousness that says, "I am the resurrection and the life." This consciousness of Life Eternal he guards as a sacred trust; his life, in its fruits of service and good deeds, daily testifies to others of the power of the Christic Consciousness.

This is the life in its higher and most holy manifestation; this is science. In every case where the Law is faithfully obeyed, results are certain; this is philosophy; it is basic religion. It concerns not merely the soul, but the body as well; it is what God has tried to teach His children, lo, these many ages.

.   "He that believeth and liveth in me"—that is, he who has faith in the God-given Law and lives accordingly—shall be free from sin, sickness, weakness, and failure, and shall demonstrate power over the last great enemy; thus shall man glorify God by living the life He had intended man to live, the end of which is happiness, peace, and contentment; making Health certain.

Chapter Eight

God With His Own

If man rightly appreciated the saying, "God helps those who help themselves," he would make greater effort toward the accomplishment of his desires. This saying actually means that God is with those who are with Him; although it must not be construed that He is against those who are not with Him in thought and in deed, nevertheless He is unable to help them.

In its literalness, this interpretation may appear to portray God as a personal being who arbitrarily refuses to help those who do not help themselves. The expression, however, is to be thought of, rather, as a literary cloak which covers a general, universal truth. Those who help themselves, by that very act, open their entire nature to receive the forces and the potencies of the Infinite. By such attitude of mind, they admit into their being the qualities that builds for success in the channels of their endeavor; they come into harmony with the Divine Law of their own being, and draw to themselves the forces that make Health certain.

Beyond successful contradiction, it may be maintained that the best way to help ourselves is to seek the *source* within of strength and power, and to co-operate with the Law governing. In the accomplishment of any worthy purpose, the first step of importance is to seek the Kingdom within; there receiving the strength and the wisdom which will enable us to work in harmony with the Law. Having obtained knowledge of truth and faith in the promise that God helps those who help themselves, it remains for us to put forth every effort in harmony with this knowledge, and to work according to our faith. This is to work in harmony with the Will of God; it is to *be with God;*

and He, being just and absolute, can not do otherwise than be with us. The result in the end, will be, that we obtain the fulfillment of our desire. This is literally true, no matter what our longing may be, whether for health of body, brilliancy of mind, or illumination of soul; or for freedom from sorrow and suffering. To be sure, none can throw off the shackles of bondage unless they attain the knowledge of cause and effect, removing the cause which produces the undesirable penalties.

In the effort to attain perfection we are not alone, for on every side there are those who are striving for the goal; many of whom have already advanced to an appreciable degree toward an ideal state of mind, body, or soul; though seldom one who is actually making any great progress in all three departments of his nature. Those who have partially achieved in one of the departments serve as examples and inspiration to others.

One should aim after the three-fold development, a perfection of body, mind, and soul; this is the only correct standard. The ideal is unity out of the trinity, one through the three.

Through knowledge of the Divine Law and obedience to it, we free the mind from thoughts and desires hampering and preventing it from greater achievement. In place of undesirable thoughts and erroneous precepts, we should think constructively, and instill exalted ideals; this will help develop the three departments of man's nature. By freeing the mind of all that retards its growth, binding it to earth, and by the establishment of powerful wholesome (holy) thoughts, we build the healthy body, the enlightened mind, and the awakened soul.

God helps those who, appreciating that His work is perfect in every sphere of action, follow the example of those who have attained. He helps those who apply to their own personality the principles and the laws demonstrated by others who have achieved. Gradually and in natural order, the personality gives birth to the individuality, and this, in turn, to Sonship with the Father and inheritance of all that rightly belongs to a son. The fact that some have attained perfection is proof that others may. In the very beginning, all creatures, including man, were faultless; but he, having free-will, has brought degradation into the universe. At last men are awakening to this truth; and, gaining an understanding of the ultimate law, and sensing perfect works, commencing to pattern after them.

Achievement is not possible in a moment; it requires time to bring about satisfactory results; but unlike all else in nature, man can exchange the carnal self for the spiritual within a comparatively short time. Even his body may be entirely reconstructed, and every cell thereof replaced with a new one. In animal life there is a constant replacement of old cells by new; but in human life, there is the added responsibility of charging, or *transfusing*, the new cells with thoughts of regeneration, perfection, and deathlessness. None other in nature has possibilities as has man. This in itself is indicative of the mighty responsibility resting upon him; proportionate to the capabilities God has given him.

No service is of greater importance at the present moment than to awaken man to his infinite possibilities; arousing in him an earnest desire to reach the highest of which he is capable. He must be brought to a realization that the life he is now living is not the most elevating; nor the one to give him the greatest power and freedom from suffering and undesirable conditions. Existing in ease, sin, and pleasure may appear to be most desirable; in reality, however, this is a delusion;

due to the universal—and misleading—thought that the downward path is easiest to travel; while destructive habits are more pleasurable than constructive and power-creating ones. Like the belief in the necessity of sickness and death, it is a race delusion which has no foundation in fact.

Another error kindred to the above and which must be eliminated entirely from man's nature, is the one leading him to believe all things that give pleasure or bring joy are evil and of the devil, and not to be indulged in. Man in his normal condition is a pleasure-loving, joy-seeking creature, naturally and instinctively craving all that induces the sensation of joy and wellbeing. Going to extremes in gratifying his fondness for sensations, or indulging in sense-delights contrary to nature's laws, will react upon him, and he reaps the after-effects; these are sorrow and suffering; consequently he concludes that everything giving pleasure or bringing joy is in itself wrong; this is an erroneous conclusion, and must be eradicated from the mind. Sorrow and suffering are not due to the gratification of sense-pleasure, but to excess, abuse, or to abnormal and illegitimate relationships.

God helps those who help themselves. He helps those who eliminate from their mental concepts false conclusions and erroneous standards; He is with all who attempt to free themselves from bondage to race beliefs.

We maintain that God judges by results and ultimate effects; He has not endowed man with pleasure-loving inclinations for the sake of taunting him through forbidding non-gratification, or for the pleasure of placing temptations in his way as a means of testing his strength. All that gives pleasure, joy, and happiness may not in themselves be evil and the gratification of sense delights is not necessarily productive of pain and sorrow. The demands of the physical nature are in themselves legitimate; aye, more than this, they are requisites of spiritual growth; agents of regeneration; necessary factors in refining and in purifying the physical organism, which in turn acts as a refining and rejuvenating force in the development of soul and overcoming weakness.

Man must learn to help himself by seeking to root out of his nature the false impression that gratification of the senses is in itself sinful. God's interest is in whether results are constructive or destructive; if the end is sorrow, pain, or loss to the self or to any other creature. When the consummation is good, constructive, and uplifting, there is no pleasure, happiness, or enjoyment, which is prohibited, nor does it in any wise meet with the disapproval of the Divine Law. The understanding of this law, and a recognition of the fact that physical welfare and normal physical satisfaction are essential to mental and spiritual well-being, gives to life a brighter hue and relieves the sombre effects of a perverted religious standard. Existence would appear far different to the vast multitudes if they could comprehend the distinction between natural use of the functions, which offers happiness, and the abnormal or perverted exercise, resulting in pain and regret. It is only man's foolish acts, his ignorance and his misconceptions of life that bring pain, sorrow, and misery into the world. Life will seem worth the living when God helps men because man helps himself by eliminating from his mind false impressions and delusive standards.

God is not attempting to place all possible pain, sorrow, and suffering upon humankind; on the contrary, He is trying to help man toward perfection, to become truly man thereby he may become as one of the gods. It is the Divine purpose that man, through evolving and developing his own inherent possibilities, shall attain unto Conscious Individuality. The pain, sorrow, and suffering which man experiences in life are not to be traced to God in any other sense than that He has given man free will; and, through perversion and misuse man has brought sorrow, suffering, and every conceivable misery upon himself and others. He who seeks wisdom that he may intelligently use his free-will is helping himself in such manner that he can truly receive the help of the Creator; God is with man when he requests help and guidance; with him when he opens the channels of his being to the Divine Presence; this assures success and is making Health certain.

Through the past centuries, God has permitted perfect beings, those who had achieved Conscious Individuality and Sonship, to teach men the "Truth, the Way, and the Life," but mankind has generally refused to listen to their voice. The last of the great Initiate-teachers who came to earth not merely taught Immortality of Soul; he demonstrated the possibility of health and strength, success and enlightenment, here and now. it has required well nigh two thousand years for man to actually begin to comprehend his possibilities. At last a few understand this seeming mystery, and *know* that mere faith in a teacher or master, no matter how infallible he may have been, will bring no results; but that it is necessary to have faith in the law he obeyed, and to live in accordance therewith. Man may have a faith that precludes the shadow of a doubt in a great Master; he may believe implicitly that another has attained Sonship with the Father and found the Christos; but it avails him nothing; is of no practical value to him unless he realizes that it is the Divine purpose for himself and all men to attain a like degree of Divinity.

The race error to be overcome—the belief that Jesus was

a miraculous exception to the generalities of humankind, that he was God come to the earth in a manner that transcends human endeavor; this delusion must be supplanted by the conviction that Jesus was an ideal illustration of what all men may attain by obeying the immutable laws as did he. He stands forth as an example, forever proclaiming to all, "What I have done ye may do." It is the divine will and purpose for all men to strive to achieve the mastery Jesus demonstrated. The Divine Presence overshadows and helps those who cherish for themselves the ideal of self-mastery. Man may work with God, be with Him, and reap actual results when he strives to live in service to others and in harmony with the Ideal; aye, he is working with God who strives to free himself from bondage to erroneous race beliefs.

Jesus, like other philosophers before his time, did not merely teach salvation of soul, as so many seem to think, he taught the idealistic development of body as well, a conscious evolution giving man health, strength, success, and power. It has required these many centuries for men to finally comprehend what Immortality really means; possibly it will be several more centuries before men will be able to transmute the race belief in sin, sickness, and death, to the greater faith; because the race mind is thoroughly saturated with the belief that sin, suffering, sickness, sorrow, and misery are unavoidable; this old conviction is in every cell of the entire body, and new cells in the process of building are charged with the same destructive thought; thus body, mind, and soul are magnetized with emotions of disease, suffering, fear, and death. "As a man thinketh in his heart;" is it any wonder that years, even centuries, are required to transmute race error into race truths?

Many who have been taught the New Commandment are

beginning to think and to live in harmony with the new, constructive ideas. The fact that physical rejuvenation and purification are essential to the spiritual growth that leads to Conscious Individuality is becoming fully understood and accepted by many. Thus, through the advanced thought and the higher understanding of the many, the race consciousness is being rapidly tinged and colored with the bright hues of belief in Immortality and physical perfection. These that believe are seeking manifestation of their own Sonship with the Father; they are practicing the precepts of this religion and philosophy whereby to attain Conscious Individuality. Many have faced the Altar Fire and gazed into the brilliant depths of their own being, and, awe-inspired by the Divine Presence, have breathed upon their own consciousness the truth, "I am the Resurrection and the Life." Upon these the Dove of Peace has alighted; and the Invisible Voice has spoken: "Thou art my beloved son in whom I am well pleased."

This consciousness of the Divine Presence; the Realization of the Ineffable Light of Immortality; and the Manifestation of physical Rejuvenation belongs to these only—a sacred trust uncommunicable to others, an exalted reality that cannot be imparted to the vast multitudes who cry out for signs and wonders.

It is a truth of paramount importance that manifestation of the Immortality of the Soul cannot be given to others, for the reason that man cannot comprehend or behold in others that which is not yet born in himself. Though a man might have reached Regeneration, have wrought his soul into a self-conscious entity, aye, even though the Holy Fire have become visible to those who have not yet reached Rejuvenation, they could not understand and would disbelieve; would consider it a delusion of the senses and not an actual fact. *Those who demand of*

others a manifestation of the Soul, of the Sacred Fire, are them-
selves yet in darkness and know neither their own real selves
nor God. Because of their blindness and misapprehension of the
truth, they demand signs and wonders, manifestations and
proofs. Their own unbelief and unworthiness have prevented
them from bringing into life the Divine Fire within themselves.

Unless we seek, and find, within ourselves, we are unable
to see, understand, and apprehend that which is within others.
Men judge others not by what they are, but by what they themselves feel, and have become in their own consciousness. It is
a natural law that man cannot realize that which is not himself, and because of this men fail to believe in the Infinite's
forgiveness, until they commence to have in their own hearts forgiveness for others. In full recognition of this law, Jesus said:
"Seek ye first the Kingdom of Heaven (within yourselves) and
all things will be added unto you."

Thus, in proportion as God is with us, as we *know* him and
realize His presence, do we expect to see him in others; likewise, as we are of the world, carnal and selfish, do we seek
to find the same unhealthy conditions in our neighbor; and fail
to understand how they can be better than we, or of greater
wisdom.

God is ever with those who are with Him. There is no
restriction placed on how much of Him we accept; nor is there
a limitation to the degree of "God in us." Man is beginning to
awaken to this truth; and overcoming the thraldom of race errors; working in harmony with the Creator and His laws, thus
making Health certain.

It is these truths that Jesus came to inculcate and to
demonstrate to mankind. Through him God proved He is with
man. By obedience to Divine Law, Jesus forshadowed the fruits

of faith when followed by works. God cannot be with those who are not with Him any more than Lazarus could go to the rich man in torment; there was a mighty, impassable gulf between them. God cannot manifest His Infinite Presence to those who claim to believe, but who in reality have little faith; there is a vast difference between profession and actual possession. God is with those who, in all humility, come to Him, asking for help, aye, even seeking for faith—more and purer faith. When the heart is sincere and in earnest, even though faith is yet weak, the true desire draws it toward God, and opens the channels to receive the influx of power from the Infinite Storehouse, this is the Path to Power; making Health certain.

Chapter Nine

Crucifixion of the Flesh

A grievous race error is apparent in the doctrine inculcating the belief that to attain eternal life it is necessary to crucify the flesh; salvation being considered impossible except through a denial of the desires native to the natural man. This dogma has undoubtedly been responsible for preventing vast multitudes from accepting the teachings of the great saviors of the past.

In its fundamental aspects, there is much truth in this conception; but it has been misinterpreted and misrepresented until the errors growing out of the misunderstanding have, in the minds of the people, totally supplanted its true significance.

From time unknown, it has been held that crucifixion of the flesh necessitates the denial of all those pleasures which are desired by the natural man—the physical creature, and this has had a tendency toward strict, severe, unreasonable self-discipline. Only a few centuries back, our puritan fathers denied their children the privilege of playing, even smiling, on the Sabbath day. Unreasonable though this may appear to the rational mind of today, to them it was the only way to please God. However, these elders were consistent; all they denied their children they proscribed for themselves. There was no legitimate cause for any such self-denial; and it is questionable whether those so strenuously careful of non-essentials in respect to Sabbath observances gave the matter serious thought. They believed in a strict observance of the written law because they themselves had been taught to uphold it; that was sufficient to them.

To us of the present age, it is given to reason and analyze; to know why an act is right or wrong. Except by a few self-righteous fanatics who would take all the joy out of life, it is not generally considered a sin to indulge in merriment and activity on the Sabbath, since our new enlightenment has taught us that man was not created for the Sabbath, but the Sabbath for man.

Determining the right or the wrong of any act in question is comparatively simple. Let the first question be, will the act bring harm or injury either to the self or to another? Let the second question be, will the act benefit anyone, either the self or another? Reasoning along these two lines will readily satisfy the most sensitive conscience in regard to the right or the wrong of a doubtful proposition.

Another important item, because it enters largely into the consideration of many acts, is whether the day on which it is committed affects the deed itself. Is it right to do a certain thing on one day or on six days, and wrong to do it on the seventh?

In general, it may be considered that what is actually wrong on the seventh day is likewise to be prohibited on any other day. The law of God is absolute in that it classifies wrong as wrong, and right as right. The Divine Fiat recognizes only two criteria for determining wrong and right; if an act, a thought, or a desire in any way results in injury to oneself or to another it is to be regarded as wrong; if it is free from injury, and beneficial to the self and others, it is to be considered as right, regardless if it be done on Wednesday or on Sunday. These two criteria are independent of days or seasons, time or place; and at once argue for man to live, think, and plan every day of the week as though it were the Sabbath day; the New Commandment maintains this to be the only true life.

As our puritan fathers had conceptions of right and wrong, as they recognized certain forms of crucifixion of the flesh, likewise, throughout the centuries, the multitudes have held various beliefs—some rational and praiseworthy, others unreasonable and often detrimental to human welfare. The irrational and the erroneous have been associated with the natural and true so intimately as to be regarded equally important. Consequently, in the minds of the masses, the errors and the falsities of the race beliefs in crucifixion of the flesh give the most prominent coloring to the doctrine, making it unattractive and even obnoxious to them. It is not surprising that the doctrine of the crucifixion of the flesh should, in the minds of the many, identify itself with an irksome self-denial, interfering with happiness and enjoyment of every description, having no foundation in reason. One cannot wonder at the rejection of the teachings of the masters and philosophers on this subject; and that, at the very mention of the word, without investigation, it is taken for granted that crucifixion embraces painful repression, merciless rigidity of discipline; and sanctimonious effacement of joy and pleasure.

That the foregoing is not a correct interpretation of the tenet of the crucifixion of the flesh as a fundamental principle is unquestionable. On the contrary, the doctrine, truly understood, admitting of bright colors and pleasing outlines is a truth that we wish to emphasize. To re-establish the Christic significance of this crucifixion in its simplicity and beauty is distinctly one of the aims of the New Commandment. We would disentangle the erroneous from the true; the irrational from the rational; and accomplish this, not by exercising priestly author-

ity in laying down definite rules of right and wrong, not by speci-
fying details for every-day use of all men alike, nor sitting in
judgment over others—far from it—but by defining general
principles through which each one may determine for himself
the right or the wrong of all that concerns his own personal life.

Crucifixion is not to be identified with repression of natural-
ness and ease, nor with the suppression of joy and merriment.
It is not in any way inconsistent with happiness and pleasure,
whether in the form of social functions, games, sports, and other
forms of wholesome recreation and diversions. Normal gratification of one's social nature, and the satisfaction of the demand
for physical activity apart from labor and toil, reasonable in-
dulgence in festivities and merry-making, stimulating interests
which admit of variety along lines of art, nature, and music—
all these are not only permissible but even advantageous to man's
spiritual growth.

This postulate the New Interpretation advocates with positive emphasis, that the rightness or the wrongfulness of a
thought, desire or an act, is to be determined by its effects or its
tendencies, whether it results in harm and injury, or in benefit
and profit, respectively to the actor and those acted upon. Any
merriment or pleasure, aye, even a thought or desire, that brings
pain, sorrow, suffering, harm, or injury to another human creature or to the participant is to be classed among "things forbidden." Nor is there any other law under the sun that classifies thought, desire, or act among the "thou shalt not." The
reason for this is not that it falls in any particular category of
usually labelled "thus shalt thou not," but under the one simple,
yet fundamental reason that it is productive of harm, therefore
destructive.

The Law which classifies as right that which is productive

of good and beneficence, and as wrong all that may bring harm and injury—this law concerns the body and everything which affects its formation; likewise all that man partakes of as food and drink; and includes hygienic laws in every department of life. Many of those who are devoutly conscientious in regard to the outer forms of worship and to visible signs of correct conduct, are, nevertheless, woefully indifferent to hygienic surroundings which vitally affect the welfare of body, mind, and *soul*. That natural laws, or those governing health and efficiency, come under the provisions of "right and wrong" is a fact that fails to arouse the conscience of many who are in other respects irreproachable in character; yet these are the important factors that we emphasize and observe, thus making Health certain.

Upon this foundation the Humanitarians rear their structure, building upon the corner stone of general principles and fundamental laws, which each *devotee* must learn to apply to his own needs as the mathematician handles his instruments. Beauty and perfection in the mathematician's work are due to an exact comprehension of laws governing his art, as well as to accuracy, precision, and delicacy in the guiding of the instruments. In like manner, beauty and perfection of character result from correct knowledge of natural and divine law, whereby one is enabled to exercise judgment and decision.

In these respects, the New Commandment departs from the well-trodden path of tradition and ancestral training; regarding natural law, that phase concerning physical health and mental efficiency, as being co-equal with ethical and moral law; in placing hygiene and dietary discretion on a par with social and moral uprightness. It extends the boundary line of righteousness to include the practical aspects of dietetics, sleep, work, exercise, and other hygienic laws, as well as the principles of eugenics and sexual exercise. We maintain that the science of Life and Immortality includes every department of man's nature—body, mind, spirit, and soul; thus, every feature of daily living that is capable of affecting his welfare in any one of these departments comes within the legitimate domain of a full and satisfying philosophy or religion. Nor is either religion or philosophy dishonored or degraded by being extended to include the practical aspects of man's four-fold being.

In respect to the doctrine of crucifixion of the flesh, adherents of the New Commandment encourage many items which are curtailed in the ordinary religious body; and discourage others which are highly regarded by formal religious sects. Particularly is this true in applying the criteria of right and wrong to the domain of food and drink. Many a devoted worshipper would shudder at the very intimation of violating a single rule of ethics or morality, yet smile in derision at the mention of a philosophy that places discretion in regard to food and drink on a par with good judgment in respect to moral conduct.

Actually, why should there be a recognition of one law for man's moral nature and another for his physical being? The same law that bases right on the foundation of beneficence and profit, and wrong on the principle of harm and injury, in the domain of ethical culture and moral conduct is *the* Law that obtains on the plane of physical welfare. The thought, word, desire, or deed that is productive of harm and injury either to the participant or to another is to be avoided; while those that are productive of positive good and helpfulness either to the participant or to another, provided it is free from harm to anyone, is to be encouraged. Similarly, food or drink which proves injurious to the physical being is to be avoided; no matter how pleasant it may be to the taste; because if it retards physical functioning and interferes with normal activity of the organism in any way; or induces poisonous accretions; stimulating appetite to an abnormal degree, it dulls or deadens the mental faculties and *directly influences the spiritual part of man.*

The religious devotee to the way of righteousness must learn to respect and to honor in his own life the laws of health and efficiency with as much devotion as he observes moral and ethical requirements, equally with the laws governing prayer, sacred silence, and meditation. To the exoteric as to the esoteric he must pay his respects with equal reverence, the outer as well as the inner, must be consulted and homage rendered. "As the outer, so the inner," is the Law of Hermes, the Thrice Wise.

It is a principle not to be ignored that physical perfection, or the refinement and the purification of physical atoms, proceeds step by step with spiritual regeneration, or Immortalization of the soul. Thus, the illumination of the soul depends upon the rejuvenation of the body. To indulge deliberately and wilfully in habits that result in sorrow, sickness, misery, regret, and inefficiency is to be accounted a sin as grievous as violation of the law which commands, "Thou shalt not kill." It may seem harsh and radical to claim that deliberate and wilful harm or injury to the body, which weakens it or shortens the earth life, is to be classed as a form of suicide; but the day is not far distant when the principle that identifies physical righteousness with moral uprightness will have become thoroughly established in the race consciousness. When the sun arises on that day man will honor spiritual and natural law with equal veneration.

Another error in connection with the law of crucifixion is the peculiar idea that in self-denial itself there is virtue, regardless of any legitimate reason for it. Test of strength, proof of unselfishness, to deny oneself that which is particularly desirable. The greater the pleasure withheld, the higher the honor and the glory of being able to forfeit such participation. Does the prodigal son manifest filial devotion by scorning the fatted calf, preferring to continue living on husks fit only for swine? Such penance, such self-punishment, has no place in a rational religion; it is unjust to oneself; it is a dishonor to God.

In its final analysis, the Law of Crucifixion identifies itself with the Laws of Justice, of Balance, and of Equilibrium. It prohibits *only* that which is harmful; encourages everything beneficial and helpful. It is by no means a hard and cruel master; rather, is generous and magnanimous in the extreme to all who honor and obey its dictates in the spirit of humility and love.

The highest aspect, however, of crucifixion of the flesh is still to be considered. Materially and spiritually, it has only one true meaning, namely, *change,* or transmutation. It is the giving of the life of the lower for the sake of the higher; it means that, mentally, spiritually, and physically, man must *change* both body and mind from the carnal self into the purified being—a creature that obeys the laws of life. The Law of Transmutation upholds unflinchingly as its standard the aim that every thought and every act shall have as their ultimate purpose greater and more sublime life. This principle obtains on both the physical and the mental planes. To eat and to drink, to be clothed, and to breathe the breath of life, to think and to plan, to cherish and desire ideals, to toil and labor—all is actuated by the one great desire, the one motive, the one aim—*the transmutation of the lower into the higher;* of the dross into pure gold; of weakness into strength; of coarse and heavy vibrations into those fine and light; of sluggish and inactive currents into alert and rapid; *of disease into health; failure into success,* and the further transmutation of the material into the spiritual; imperfection into the flawless; irresolution into firmness of will; selfishness into generosity; malice and envy and bitterness into forgiveness and kindness and good-will; ignorance, error, and sin into knowledge, goodness, and righteousness—*this is the esoteric significance of the crucifixion.*

The orthodox interpretation has emphasized the element of denial, or "giving up." Unquestionably this is necessary, for the lower must be sacrificed for the sake of receiving the higher; but we would paint the beauty and the grandeur of the higher, that which is to be received, rather than dwell on the pain and the anguish of separation from that from which we must be parted. In its true sense, denial means death; but the mistake of the ages has been in losing sight of the *new birth that results from this death or denial.* Place emphasis on the glory of the New Life, and the travail of birth is quickly forgotten; paint in life-like colors the rose-tinted sunrise glow of the new morning, and the darkness of the darkest hour is soon lost to memory.

Let us remember that in the process of passing from the lower to the higher, from the carnal to the spiritual, there is death or crucifixion only to the undesirable. The truly valuable is not to be transmuted; because there is no law, either natural or divine, that calls for denial of that which is of permanent value. Many things in life, nevertheless, are of worth only as an object for exchange; and the real value of many so-called blessings consist in their ability to be transmuted into something of greater service. Silver or golden coin are neither food nor drink; not an ornament to the body nor a joy to the intellect, nevertheless are of value because they can readily be trans-

formed (exchanged) for these. According to the Law of Crucifixion, that upon which is passed the penalty of death is desirable by reason of its transmutability into something of intrinsic worth.

In this connection, let it be emphasized that normal, healthful pleasures are profitable to man as a means of stimulating the
higher forces; consequently, self-denial in regard to them de-
feats the very purpose they are intended to serve. Miserly hoard-
ing of money is self-denial in respect to expenditure; but it de-
prives the owner of the advantages to be gained by a judicious
disposition of it. Likewise, strict, rigid self-discipline which
refuses to satisfy normal, natural demands of the body or mind
may possess the virtues of self-control; but it fails to satisfy
the Law of Transmutation. Normal gratification of natural desire for pleasure, whether physical, mental, or social, is of great
worth in that it stimulates to activity forces which would otherwise lie dormant and useless. The energies thus aroused may be
directed into channels of usefulness, serving a place of untold
benefit. True self-satisfaction in respect to innocent pleasures,
therefore, consists in the attitude of mind one takes toward them;
the enlightened mind says: "I satisfy this desire not merely for
the pleasure derived from it, but especially for the sake of stimulating forces, aspirations and ambitions which I intend to turn
into channels of usefulness," thus recognizing the Law
of Transmutation. The lower motive of mere pleasure for its
own sake is crucified; more correctly speaking, it is transmuted into, or gives life to, the higher motive of receiving power
and strength and stimulus to be directed into channels of lofty
endeavor; on this principle, that legitimate joys and pleasures of
both mind and body are not only permissible, but valuable and

even necessary to the highest culture, the New Commandment places great emphasis.

It is equally true that many things in themselves desirable, as pleasures and joys, the means of awakening dormant forces and potencies in one's life, serve as a medium of transmutation; and it is a fact that normal gratification of these satisfy the Law of Crucifixion of the flesh when the lower motive is sacrificed to the higher aspiration. However, it is not to be forgotten that there are many undesirable traits and qualities which must be overcome; and the sacrifice of transmutation of these is another form of satisfying this law. There are many desires and tendencies which must be refused; and the foregoing of such gratification is one form of crucifixion. There are many habits thoroughly established in one's nature which must be corrected; and the rectification of harmful habits is also a feature of this law.

Chief among the undesirable tendencies is that of harboring destructive thoughts and feelings; man must overcome and change, he must transmute these into that which is desirable; such a denial requires strength, and often the execution is painful; but he who holds to the ideal standard of healthful, constructive thought will count suffering as nothing in comparison with the gain to be derived therefrom.

Most deadly among the degrading passions is the tendency to anger; this must be overcome; it manufactures a poison which inoculates both mind and body. No one really wishes to give way to a fit of anger, but the habit may gain such power over one as to seem uncontrollable; let him who is a slave to this passion take courage; it is possible to transmute it into a power for good, anger being the antithesis of forgiveness. The force expended in the direction of anger and malice may be turned into the channel of good-will and wholesome service. It is much like an uncontrolled current of water; by harnessing it and utilizing it in running your machinery, it is transformed from a source of danger and menace into a benefit. The force and power manifested in anger is good; overcome the tendency, change the current, set it to work running your physical and mental machinery according to the ideal of service to others; and you transmute its power into strength, making Health certain.

Admittedly, overcoming the tendency to anger and quick judgment calls for great watchfulness and persistent effort; but the greater the price paid, the more desirable the reward. When the passion manifests, immediately make conscious effort to change it into good-will, forgiveness, and love. This requires extreme will-power, courage and persistency; it is a real crucifixion; it is difficult and painful, the passion being part of one's very life.

Jealousy is the twin to anger; of the vast multitudes very few are free from this monster. Here is a mighty work to be accomplished; a crucifixon that will be deeply felt; a powerful current of force which must be changed. Nevertheless, great is the reward of those who overcome; desirable the price of victory; and glorious the crown of the champion. If it is a matter of jealousy because of possessions, one must control one's thought and wish another no less, though being justified in desiring more for oneself; providing legitimate effort is made to obtain that wanted or needed. The energy wasted in begrudging and jealousy when turned into honest endeavor, quickly helps us to achieve.

Envy, the master of countless numbers, offers great opportunity for crucifixion. Within most people this passion has a strong hold. It is difficult for these to understand why others, apparently not as worthy, not laboring as hard as they, should have greater possessions. We forget that the soul has existed eternally and made many pilgrimages, and possibly the one we envy may have suffered greatly and earned fully all it has. Envy must be crucified; we must *change* it into love, must desire happiness for those whom we are tempted to envy.

Thus we see that crucifixion is real and that there is necessity for it in the lives of all men and women. Crucifixion, however, is not a process of stifling, stultifying, or destroying; this statement is true both in regard to natural, normal desires, passions, and appetites, whether of body, mind, or soul, which may be gratified, and in respect to undesirable traits, qualities and tendencies, which are to be overcome, or *changed*. Crucifixion is not a negative process, it is always a positive, active labor. In the case of destructive traits it is the art of changing them consciously into constructive habits; while in respect to innocent pleasures, it is the art of transmuting the thought of mere pleasure into that of awakening forces to be employed in channels for good. In either case, it demands alertness and activity. The old idea of self-denial results in sluggishness and weakness of character; but an understanding of the Christic Interpretation is productive of power, strength, life—newness of life—making Health certain.

As we pass through the various states of crucifixion, we gradually free the mind from bondage and the fetters that bind it—as with rods of iron. Thus, having obtained freedom for the mind from undesirable, destructive passions, we are at leisure to devote time to pursuits and interests that are pleasure-bringing and constructive. As these changes continue, the body eliminates the deadly poisons which had been previously generated. As body and mind gain strength, the soul awakens and is enlightened; unfoldment and development follows. Gradually, mortality puts on immortality; man becomes like the gods; and, in time, Sonship with the Father is established; man has gained Conscious Individuality.

These are some of the principles underlying the doctrine of crucifixion of the flesh as taught by us. They are not presented merely with the idea of satisfying an intellectual craving for speculation in regard to doctrinal tenets; they are for those who hunger after truth, righteousness, and service; those who are anxious to apply to their own character the measuring rod of self-discipline, aye, especially for those who are ready to honor and obey the Law as a means of transmuting dross and alloy into pure gold; failure into success; weakness into strength; mortality into immortality, thereby making Health certain.

No amount of faith in the personality of Jesus as an extraordinary character, aye, not even faith in him as the only begotten Son of God and as one arisen from the dead, can suffice to redeem man from the bondage of ignorance, error, and sin. Faith, however, in the law he obeyed in demonstrating Sonship with the Father and power over death—this will accomplish wonders in redeeming man from bondage to ignorance, error, and sin, *if daily lived.* Jesus *was* a deliverer in that he taught a doctrine and a system of living which will, when obeyed, free mankind from ignorance, sickness, and failure.

Chapter Ten

Is Life Without Religion Human?

The frequently repeated assertion that religion is not essential to the higher life of people, the same height in culture and enlightenment being attainable, and life as desirable, without religion; is always based on ignorance or a wilful perversion of truth.

Seemingly, this is an age of irreligion; but underneath the surface, beneath the seeming contempt for all apparently religious, there is in the hearts of man, lying dormant perhaps, a respect for true worship as pronounced as ever found in the souls of men in any age. Undoubtedly it is true that men have lost respect for formal homage to a personal duty; and no longer accept the current interpretation of the Biblical narrative; and have ceased to respect the established church; as also the various vehicles through which spiritual formulas are given the people; but one can no longer wonder at this, considering the fanaticism of bigoted formalists who are attempting to force men to attend church, whether they will or not; and who, if successful in securing legislative enactments, will do more to breed discontent, irreligion, and disgust with law and order among the people, than would world economic conditions.

Religion is life itself; without it man would quickly degenerate to the status of the animal. It is the link connecting man with the higher spheres; if this be broken man loses his birthright; becoming less human than the savage; for the say-age, though illiterate and uncultured, according to our standard, has a comprehensive religion.

There are men who maintain they have faith in no religion bcause they do not even believe in the existence of a God: but give heed to the man who voices such a claim, as he proceeds with his duties, and his business relations with his fellow men. Question him carefully, and you may find that his religion. is work, a method of business. He deals honestly with all men in his transactions, though there is no outer restraint to compel him to practice fair methods. Ask him why he does so, and he will inform you that he considers it best. Tell him that as he believes in nothing, there is neither external nor internal law to compel him to be honest, why not take advantage of this and accrue power and influence, as well as money, through selfish and illegitimate means? The usual answer to such a question is: "No, I think honesty is best." He may be unconscious of the fact, nevertheless, honesty is to him a religion; and he lives it faithfully; nor is the spiritual feeling within him dead; it simply does not exhibit itself as such because he has not found a satisfactory avenue of expression. How much more desirable to both God and man is such a life than that of the one who professes the salvation of his soul, as also close relationship with God, but whose word is never to be depended upon, while his business methods always require careful watching?

Theorize as we may, religion is the only reality there is. It is not a mere belief, nor a blind faith; but *living in obedience to the divine will*, It is founded on the principle of life; is the incentive back of life; the *divine urge* that called man into being. It is the link between man and God; and when man attempts to actually free himself from the bond he quickly degenerates lower than the brute.

Proportionate as man has this religious consciousness within him will be his love for all that is worth while in life. Prayer and devotion to formal worship are not the only means whereby man expresses his spiritual emotions; on the contrary, the most perfect manifestation of religious sentiment is in the love of the beautiful and flawless. Love of flowers, of music, of art, of architecture, of symmetry and proportion, all these are evidence of a devotional nature. Religion may be aptly defined as love for all that is beautiful; the beauty that is the natural result of perfection and harmonious with it; and according to the religious feeling and sentiment in one's nature will be the devotion to the various expressions of beauty and perfection.

It is an established fact, known to all close observers, that men who are the most truly spiritual in their nature are the greatest lovers of music, flowers, the arts, and of the aesthetic in all departments of life; nor should one be led to believe that this fondness for the beautiful need lead away from the practical and useful; utility and true beauty going hand in hand. Beauty is another synonym for perfection; the highly bred animal is a perfect specimen of its kind; the loveliest flower is the most exquisite of its kind; flawlessness in the equipment of a building is inseparable from the purpose it is intended to serve; the noble character is an example of grace and virtue; while the splendid physique is a picture of health as well as a dream of pleasing outlines; in fact, *health is the secret of beauty, both in form and feature.* In reality, in the final analysis, religious sentiment and love of the beautiful and exquisite are synonymous terms.

Beyond all contradiction, religion has but one aim—the perfection of man. This is not a formal faith; but a feeling; not a formulated belief, but a desire for the highest attainment; not a profession of faith in some creed, but a Spiritual light in

the heart of man. It is a delight in the noble and beautiful
wherever found; a faith in the ultimate ideal wherever manifested. Its highest expression is in the love for one's fellow
men, and in the labor of developing manhood or womanhood in
its highest phase. The incentive for the realization of ultimate
perfection as the goal placed before man and woman, is the
evidence of true religion; while faith and effort in its attainment
is the proof of godly devotion. A purpose and a will-power that
draws one constantly toward the ideal in every department of
life, is uncontradictory evidence of religion's power and fervor.

It is a delusive idea that would lead us to believe true faith
is dead in the present age; that men are irreligious at heart
is a grievous misconception of facts. At no time in the history
of the world have men desired more for the harmonious and
beautiful as expressions of higher development than in the present age. Evidence of this is readily recognized in the tendency
of the time toward the elevation and spiritualization of the various arts and trades, crafts and professions. Some are devoted to
the greater improvement of all constructive machinery; others
to the purpose of developing the plant, fruit, and flower; and
many to breeding stock to its highest purity; all these are engaged
in elevating pursuits, and the incentive is the internal urge
having its foundation in a love for the ideal. Admittedly an ever
increasing number are leaving the church; but this is not the indication of an inclination to become less religious, rather is it to
be considered as silent testimony of their loss of faith in the
churches as dependable institutions; and creeds as saviors of
souls; all this due to their experiences with men who loudly
profess religion while profiteering in business and exploiting
women and children; and with others who confess great liber-
ality of thought at one moment and are in readiness to persecute

and prosecute those who differ with them; or with others who continuously make various promises and never fulfill any of them, and do not even possess the manhood or courtesy to inform the promisee to the contrary.

In the trades and business activities, the modern spirit presents the appearance of rivalry and competition, and this serves as a goad that stimulates men to more skilled execution and greater effort. Rivalry is an incentive toward accuracy and delicacy—another form of idealism. The universal demand for superior goods and more excellent workmanship incites to genuine love for quality and unquestionable skill in the preparation of products. Even the struggle for existence arouses latent forces and unrecognized abilities in the expression of artistic tendencies. It is freely admitted that economic conditions today are far from ideal, due to the profiteering of a favored few of those in possession of wealth, and an attempt to imitate these unholy ones by multitudes of workers jealous of the power of the few; and that often rivalry and competition do not germinate in altruistic motives; nevertheless, despite unjust conditions and cruel measures, spiritual feelings throb under the tattered garb of many a humble workman who honors the ideal in doing his best in every undertaking; as well as under the silks and satins of the ultra-rich who recognize their possessions only as an avenue through which to benefit mankind generally. Many a lad, born with the instinct of the beautiful, forced by poverty to a life of toil, finds satisfaction in giving artistic expression and willing execution to the task in hand. This may be commonplace duty; his implements may be crude; but he honors both the labor and the instruments by the accuracy of his skill in the accomplishment; so he satisfies a deeply-rooted religious instinct, although he may actually consider himself an unbeliever and agnostic.

The present is the age wherein love of the beautiful and harmonious are made practical and useful. It is no longer considered that one who delights in the esthetic sits with folded hands dreaming of heavenly chants and music of harps; on the contrary, he is satisfied with no less than the actual creation or expression of the beauty he feels. If circumstances debar him from discovering an outlet for his artistic tendencies in the channels of his choice, *he quickly applies his love of harmony and symmetry to the task at hand;* and through faithful performance of commonplace duties according to a lofty ideal, *he creates for himself an avenue along the lines of his choice.* Eventually he becomes master of his art, and gives expression to the dreams of his childhood, *this is the path to success.*

Undoubtedly men no longer give the expression to religious feeling in the same manner they did formerly. Long, tiresome lip prayers fail to satisfy; sermons the length of which are measured by hours, are losing their influence over men. However, often those who find religious forms and ceremonies irksome are generous in expressing their appreciation of the beautiful and perfect wherever found; are unrestrained in their praise of inspiring, soul-stirring music and art; and are held enraptured by the power of harmony and rhythm in sound, color, and movement. They are liberal to the highest degree when an appeal is made to their generosity for money to benefit the needy; and ever ready with the helping hand when a fallen brother or sister requires their assistance, morally, spiritually, or financially. *This is true worship at the shrine of God.*

The religion of the people is taking practical form; demanding positive expression, this is an encouraging sign. Men are becoming lovers of perfection in every department of life; great is the mystery indicated by this truth. *Love of the ideal, in time, will induce men to seek this state for themselves. Herein we read the handwriting on the wall, the coming of an enlightened period, which is to be when religion shall have become the life of the people—an existence the aim of which is the equal development and refinement—an exaltation of body, mind, and soul.*

For this reason the New Commandment encourages men seeking the beautiful; those attempting the achievement of perfection for its own sake, and surrounding themselves with the best and highest in art. We may not be able to lead men at one bound to accept the exalted life and the ultimate aim of religion —*the deification of manhood and womanhood;* but by giving them the most sublime expressions of art and nature, we stimulate in them energies which tend eventually toward the ideal race. The more the individual is encouraged in the gratification of that phase of the idealistically practical which he most desires, the quicker will be his response to the appeal for the personification of all that is exalted. To argue that love for the beauties of nature, God's handiwork, is not a type of worship, is to deny that the letter, *a,* is a part of the alphabet.

Veneration for that which is perfect and a desire to express it is the attracting center to which all men are being drawn. God Himself is revealed to mankind through the beauties of His creation. The nearer faultless an object is, the more closely it resembles God—the one epithet applied to God being *perfection.* Love of the exquisite in the heart of any one gives evidence that there is therein a desire for God and all that pertains to Him, and requires merely the arousing of the Spark of Divinity when it will burst into a flame; sweeping all before it. Find a

man who cares little for music, who lacks interest in the beautiful, whose heart remains unstirred by tokens of perfection, and
you have a creature who cares little for life, and less for
the love of his fellow men—*Religion is not in the heart*. He is in
reality no longer man; but a broken reed shaken and tossed and
blown here and there by every wind.

A growing desire for the beautiful and flawless gradually
awakens in the heart of man a something of which he was heretofore unaware. This manifests itself in the longing to become worthy of all that is of intrinsic value; to harmonize with,
and become part of it. This new birth will, in the beginning,
create a restlessness, possibly an indescribable hunger of the
heart, a yearning, leading to the search for that which will satisfy. In some manner, man should, at this stage of his growth,
be induced to recognize that *all* for which he longs—all beauty,
all power, all energy, all harmony, all of creative potency, are to
be found *within* himself. The method of realization should be
clearly indicated to him; if he will *live*, the desire will gradually
become as a *living fire* sweeping all before it, then it will become
apparent to him that love of the beautiful and noble constitutes
religion the most sincere and devout. Though it may manifest
first as a passion for music and harmony, or for the beauties of
nature, or a desire for health and strength, in the end it becomes
a passion for regeneration and rejuvenation of the self—a burning urge to become like the Father.

Mankind has been passing through various stages of
growth; leading to the place whence real progress may be made.
The turning point has been reached; and definite growth noted.
But a few centuries ago, men lived in self-denial; not in respect
to that which it is well to exercise self-control, but in suppressing every expression of love for the beautiful. It was for-

bidden to be surrounded with objects of beauty; many harbored the belief that music should be discouraged; laughter was God-forbidden; asceticism, rather than religion, prevailed; even now a few sects may be found who forbid household adornments and the beautiful in dress. Denial and repression originates in regard for a creed, *rather than in love for an ideal.* In the hearts of men there was not so much love, joy and peace, as in the hearts of those who today profess no religion, or church connection, but who surround themselves with the beautiful; cherishing lofty ideals, and generous, kindly thoughts. Many of those who today are classed as irreligious and non-believers in respect to outer forms of worship have in their hearts less hatred, jealousy, envy, and ill-will than those who make loud profession of faith. In the early days of American history religious zeal led men to persecute and even burn those whom they looked upon as heretics; and it is evident that, although men of our day do not make much public confession of faith, and consequently considered less religious, they are, in fact, more truly spiritual, and less in bondage to destructive passions, while fellowship has a stronger place in their hearts.

Progress is marked; nevertheless, this is merely the awakening stage in the growth of the race; shortly will come the actual developing stage, wherein men will actively seek to find all that will give life more abundantly; the Humanitarians foresee this and have prepared for the work. When this new age is fully come, men *will live the life of development;* will seek for Conscious Individuality; will turn failure into success; making Health certain.

Truly men have fallen from their divine estate; but that is no indication they will need remain thus; rather, having gained knowledge of their primary mistake, and wisdom helping them reclaim their heritage will press forward, onward, and upward, until the sublime realization is attained; becoming as one of the gods, knowing good from evil; choosing the constructive because of the realization that only through this is life to be found.

What was the prevailing doctrine of the age that we have just left behind; was it that man should be perfect? Was it not rather that he should subscribe to a form, that outside of this theme could be no salvation, no life in eternity? Admittedly, it was taught man should obey God or be condemned, and forever damned; but how was he to obey? In becoming like the Father, physically and spiritually, or in crucifying the flesh, destroying it, suppressing and degenerating its normal demands?

What is the fundamental of the New Commandment for the New Age?

"That man shall redeem the body and cleanse the heart." This is the foundation upon which the religion, the very life, of the new man, must be built. Not to crucify the flesh, nor to ignore it, neither to mortify the body; but to care for it, develop it, cleanse it through right living, and *regenerate it through obedience and constructive thoughts.* To perfect the body that it may become a beautiful temple wherein the soul of man manifests as the son of God—this is the doctrine of the new age.

It is two fold; it not only inculcates the upbuilding, the perfection, and the beautifying of the body, but *also to cleanse the heart.* Man must free himself of all that is destructive in thought and thereby build the Immortal Soul, attaining Conscious Individuality.

This is the basis of the religion for the age; it is practical; sanctified by God. We *know* this because those who have obeyed its instructions have found it constructive and redemptive. Its principles can be applied to every-day needs, and the reward is manifold. "Redeem the body that is thine, and cleanse the soul with the body." This is the message we bring to men. It is neither mysterious, nor hard to understand; it is life-giving and inspiring; making Health Certain.

The Exalted Life

Crucifixion is not to be identified with repression of natural-ness and ease, nor with the suppression of joy and merriment. It is not in any way inconsistent with happiness and pleasure, whether in the form of social functions, games, sports, and other forms of wholesome recreation and diversions. Normal gratifi-cation of one's social nature, and the satisfaction of the demand for physical activity apart from labor and toil, reasonable in-dulgence in festivities and merry-making, stimulating interests which admit of variety along lines of art, nature, and music— all these are not only permissible but even advantageous to man's spiritual growth.

Chapter Eleven

Man, Temple of the Living God

"Ye are the Temples of the Living God" was thundered forth by St. John, the favored apostle, and is the great Law of being. Three or more thousand years before the Christian era the world's greatest philosopher taught his students this same saving truth in the old law: "As it is below, so it is above." Likewise, "as it is above, so it is below." According to this expression of order must all that exists be considered.

What is our opinion of a building in most respects perfect, but crumbling away in spots? Its superior style of architecture, its faultless designs, and its construction are all lost to view by reason of the process of decay clearly shown. That which is inferior is always the first to attract attention; a weakness is ever the more conspicuous by virtue of its contact with the perfect.

The body of the average man is such a building; he was patterned after the image of the Creator and endowed with the same attributes. Whether we accept it or not, it is none the less true that the body of man is the temple of the living God, or else all sacred literature, including the Christian's Bible, is a fraud. As the temple of the living God man is an exact prototype of a beautiful temple structure in which men worship the Father; and though the body, this temple, may be faultless in its construction and appointments, if it is marred through the effects of disease it is not all it was intended to be; and worship therein, that is, *the expression of God,* cannot be holy (whole-ly) so long as weakness and illness is in possession.

This truth brings us face to face with a serious problem, one that affects every living being. It is this: only *one* attribute can fully manifest itself through the body at a time; therefore, the presence of disease in man is conclusive evidence that God, the Divinity, is not solely in possession of that temple; but that the carnal nature, or call it what we will, is 'the master. One or the other is always in control and predominates. God is revealed through health, beauty, and harmony; evil manifests in disease, inharmony, suffering and sin. All that is perfect is of God; and it is correct to say that evil is represented by weakness, failure, disease, and death.

Unquestionably man is the temple of the living God; but it must be acknowledged that more generally the temple is occupied by other than the Father. It is incumbent upon man to so prepare the human structure that God will gladly dwell therein; since it is· undeniable that the Infinite cannot abide unless it is fit for His presence.

This demands a consideration of the concept "Divine Being," or "the Infinite." Many do not think of the Infinite as a personal being, consequently unable to comprehend how the All-Inclusive could be in man, and skeptical as regards man being the Temple of God. Each one is free to cast aside every idea of personality and individuality in connection with Deity; but the fact remains that if we do not give proper attention to the body, if we fail to satisfy its normal requirements as regard food, clothing, sleep, exercise, and other requisites of health, strength, and success, there will be disease and failure, resulting in suffering, inharmony, distress, and inefficiency; and we say God does not dwell there. It is immaterial whether we assert;

"God does not dwell in the temple," or state that health, happiness, harmony, love, forgiveness, and freedom from suffering do not inhabit that body. If God can not dwell in the temple, then perfection does not there exist.

We believe in the existence of God as a Universal, all-embracing Intelligence and Creative Force, containing within Himself all of Love, Strength, Beauty, Power, and Infinite Energy; but instead of limiting Him to definite boundaries of time and space, of personality and individuality, we think of Him as including *all that is*. He is health. He is happiness. He is Life. He is freedom from ignorance, error, and sin. Consequently, we say that disease, inharmony, ignorance, error, and sin prevailing in the temple of flesh, is equivalent to the assertion that God does not dwell there; that Godhood has not been attained, and cannot be, while these destructive conditions predominate.

Think of a beautiful temple with perfection in detail, design, architecture, material, decorations, and appointments, and what such a temple would be worth to humanity without a God-like priest to officiate; and humble, sincere worshippers to attend. Undesirable as this would be, it is an exact symbol of the average human being. It is possible for the temple of flesh to be perfect in all its features and still be desolate and unoccupied by the Godhead; likewise is it probable for the body to be like a beautiful structure—a specimen of physical perfection, while the character dwelling within is destitute of the divine attributes. Man may be faultless as an animal, but altogether carnal; merely a temple of flesh. The body to be a highly developed animal, a beautiful temple of flesh, is truly desirable and to be encouraged; but this in itself is by no means all of life; it is *not* the divine plan and purpose for man; but rather, that he shall be both man and god; and the possibility of becoming a healthy animal, destitute of active divine attributes; of building a beautiful temple of flesh without an exalting priesthood within, this is a danger to be avoided.

In the construction of the perfect temple, man must have in view the ideal body; healthy, normal, and with great strength, free from disease and the suffering attending disease; and an exalted and illuminated soul as the occupant and ruler of it. These two ideals must proceed hand in hand, and both processes of development take place simultaneously. When the body has reached a certain stage of development the soul shall have become illumined and Conscious; then man may rest assured God dwells within the temple. If these two aspirations are constantly in mind, every cell of the physical being becomes charged with the *Divine Desire;* the body will not merely be healthy, normal flesh, but 'flesh of His flesh," and "Soul of His soul."

This two-fold process is the normal, correct temple-building. It is a method to change (transmute) the mortal into the immortal. It is not a procedure of destruction, or tearing down; but the natural rebuilding or changing, a growth as God had intended it to be; it is making Health certain.

When man has accomplished this great work, when, through his thoughts and desires and habits of living, he has changed the body from disease and suffering to health and harmony; when the mind has become awakened to the newer and greater life. and the soul enlightened and conscious—then has God in very truth come to that man and taken possession of the temple; man not only becoming the Son of God, but attaining Conscious Individuality and a co-worker with the Father.

Having passed through this inner development, a far-off heaven is non-existent, nor does he look forward to the distant event of entering a heavenly kingdom. He has entered the Elysian sphere, and clearly understands this life to be a part of the greater life, that *now* he enters into his heritage, becoming one with those others who have gone before. Heaven is *where* and *what* we make it. When Heaven commences, or how one enters it, rests entirely with the individual. At the moment we free ourselves from bondage to the undesirable and destructive we begin to live the true life, and with the new life, heaven opens to us its portals. The consciousness of life on a higher plane is heaven. Harmony and peace, loyalty to a noble ideal, to whatever degree developed, belong to that extent to heaven; there are grades of heaven as there are of consciousness and realization.

Life is a continual building. It required the entire life of King Solomon to build the great temple; in that building all the material was carefully inspected to assure it being desirable. In like manner should we give our whole attention to the material that is to build our temple; and exercise care that nothing except strong, healthy, virile cells be allowed to form the body. This necessitates constant watchfulness; our thoughts and feelings must be guarded and controlled. Thoughts and emotions of hatred, anger, ill-will, and malice must not be granted admittance to mind or heart. Cells thus charged are no more fit to enter the bodily structure than are imperfect stones in building the walls of a temple that is to endure for ages.

If, when packing a barrel of fine apples with the intention of keeping them for any length of time, one commencing to decay be accidentally left with the good, it would shortly inoculate those surrounding it; in time infecting the entire barrel. It is the same with the cells of the body; one charged with vibrations of anger will poison neighboring cells and affect the healthy ones within a short time. Cells charged with hatred and anger are destructive in their effect; consequently tearing down rather than building up the physical organism; hence a continual work of destruction proceeds in the body of man. Besides the passions mentioned, there are many others which charge the cells with a destructive force, poisoning the centers; inducing disease and abnormal conditions; making health impossible.

When we fully understand the Law governing Temple Building and have in mind that every moment in the life of man is one of construction; that not food alone is necessary in this process, but that every thought, desire, and passion is charging the physical cells with its particular type of vibrations, *then do we possess the key to life, health, and happiness.*

We wish to emphatically state that the method employed by Apollonious of Tyana, as well as by Jesus, in healing the sick, i. e., freeing man from disease, is disclosed in the foregoing statement. They taught the sufferer *how* to free the mind from the thoughts, passions and desires continually charging the cells with disease-creating vibrations; instructing them in substituting health-inducing thoughts, desires, and emotions, thereby filling each cell with vitality and the virile force essential to making Health certain.

These inculcators of a *saving* gospel fully understood that it is utterly impossible for the man who thinks only of the good, the true, and the beautiful, whose mind is filled with thoughts of love, good-fellowship, and kindness, and obeying Nature's Laws, to be diseased in mind or body; his cells, momentarily created, constantly building into the body the life-giving forces and energies; making Health certain.

The principles here advanced picture the ideal life; but let it be understood that we may possess just as much of the desirable as we are willing to make effort to obtain. In proportion we free the mind of hatred, anger, jealousy, and envy; and substitute in their place thoughts of good-will, fellowship and love will we have peace, harmony, happiness, and contentment. Results will be in ratio with the effort; and if we cleanse the mentality and the heart altogether of destructive thoughts and desires; eating life-giving foods; observing hygenic habits; we build towards perfection. The choice is ours; the work is before us; it is merely a question of how greatly we desire these blessings and what effort we are willing to put forth.

Another obstacle in the path of the great work, one that must be entirely eliminated, is the element of fear. No one can attain the highest degree of perfection so long as he allows this *depressor* to be a part of his nature. It is the greatest detriment to achievement; more paralyzing in its effects than either anger, jealousy, envy, or malice; its benumbing effect is to be accounted for in the fact that it effectively prevents us from giving up the old destructive life, and grasping hold of the new and greater, constructive life. Man is in fear constantly; he dreads the opinions of neighbors and friends; is apprehensive of being deprived of pleasures he now enjoys; is dismayed by the thought that he may be required to sacrifice profits otherwise his. He forgets for the moment that by accepting the new life he will win friends and associates of greater benefit to him than those who would deny him; that through this life new pleasures will come, far more intense than were the old; yet constructive, elevating, and free from bitter after-effects.

Fear is the shackle that binds the millions to a life of

misery, suffering, and the undesirable; a life that offers an hour
of pleasure, followed by hours or years of sorrow and pain;
is like a great black desert in the minds and hearts of the multitudes; in the soul of man like a swamp on an otherwise beautiful farm, making it but one-tenth profitable. If this unsightly
and miasmic lowland is allowed to remain it decreases even the
value of the productive soil; but if leveled with good ground
and cultivated, there will be one vast, beautiful estate. Thus
is fear in the heart of man; holding him in subjection more than
nine-tenths of his life; and the one-tenth is overshadowed by
the repressing influence of the monster.

Through comprehension of the destructive effects of fear,
and the effectual effort of closing up this miasmic swamp with
thoughts and desires for the beautiful, lovable, and true; interest and obedience to the Divine Law; a life in harmony with
Nature's dictates, may man reclaim himself; manifoldly increasing his efficiency, and making of himself a whole (holy) man.
Having obtained his freedom from the monster, he will exercise
all his faculties; rebuilding the bodily structures and becoming
the temple of the Living God; center of the measureless estate
destined to be his by·divine heritage; no longer in bondage to
suffering, pain, sorrow, failure, and weakness; but the posses-
sor of happiness, strength, health, success, and Conscious of his
Individuality; this is making Health Certain.

Chapter Twelve

Fear, Gate of Death

Fear is a destroyer of power, of energy, and of life. Has been holding the vast multitudes in a strangling grasp; forcing them to accept the same doctrines, whether true or false, as acknowledged by friends, neighbors, and instructors. Men have been afraid to do otherwise than believe that which has been taught by those in authority; as a consequence, they were deluded into the belief that their own way of thinking must be abnormal and untrustworthy; to be checked, rather than be encouraged, if their souls were to be saved. Even the few who cherished ideas of their own seldom dared to follow them as principles of life lest they be looked upon as revolutionists and out of harmony with the majority.

At last men are commencing to think for themselves; recognizing that each individual has a mind of his own *for no other reason than to use wherewith to do his own thinking.* They are beginning to understand that the new cycle with its Christic interpretation actually has for its foundation the principles of the teachers and philosophers of the past which men thought they were following; whereas, in reality, they had accepted the modern interpreters merely as external authority, and their instructions as creeds or dogmas with no adequate comprehension of their inner meaning. Men are gradually coming to a realization that the value of fundamental instructions rest in their application to the needs of daily life. To become convinced of the practical aspects of a philosophy or a system of life, is to induce one to think for himself. No one else can determine in detail the requirements of an individual life, neither can external authority solve the problems that concern that life. A great Master may interpret and expound general principles; but each individual must study, think, and contemplate for himself whereby he may obtain an intelligent comprehension of the adaptability of these principles to his daily need. Of this fact men are now being convinced; as a consequence, they pay homage to their own power of thought, though many do not yet trust in their final conclusions.

The moment man truly thinks, he commands fear to "get thee behind me, satan," and really commences to live. With thought will come newness of life; the incentive for more independent action; a longing to dare, to do, and to know. Thinking, acting, and living in harmony with the Divine Law in its own time results in a renewal of life; one that will be truly worth living. Admittedly, this new life often requires a struggle because it is not always in harmony with the ideas of those about us; this means conflict within and without; but, if the mind is fully awakened to the ideal of the regenerate life, it is not readily led astray, but persists in following the path indicated by the Law, and finds Health and success.

Fear is not life, it is death; in reality, it is hell. If there were no other law to punish us for misdeeds, fear alone would be a hades terrible enough to satisfy even the most orthodox. It is timidity that prevents man from doing his best; cowardice not to act in harmony with the inner promptings; and a living terror to be left standing outside of the fold of popular opinion. To be under the thraldom of fear is a worse bondage than the Hebrews suffered in ancient Egypt.

The Humanitarians in teaching men to free themselves from cowardice, from all undesirable conditions, and to live as they think they should, despite the opinions of men and authority-taught doctrines, if such do not harmonize with their own intuitive conceptions of the truth; though nothing in this is to be construed as to place the stamp of approval on any disrespect or disobedience to law and order. We teach men to seek their freedom from every fear, except the one, that of the action of the Divine Law when they do contrary to the dictates of their own conscience; there being no immunity when one disobeys the dictates of conscience as to what is wrong. None should fear God, for he is the God of Love, and "Perfect love casteth out all fear," but fear to dishonor and to disobey Him in this sense is to reverence and render Him homage.

There is a two-fold incentive for man to overcome the sense of dread and cowardice. First, there is freedom itself, which is a great satisfaction and brings peace and well-being. Second, the realization that the weakness may be transmuted into power: Thus the method of overcoming is both positive and negative; it insures the lifting of the burden from an undesirable and destructive state of mind; and, in addition, confers a positive, active energy to take the place of the unholy emotion.

Fear is to be overcome through the Law of Transmutation; the force expended or wasted in this negative state is to be changed into power for good, wherewith to accomplish and achieve. Every passion known to man, every chain and bond that binds him, *when changed,* becomes an *active* agent for good. For this reason, among others, the New Commandment does not advocate the destruction, or killing, or suppression, of any passion or tendency, no matter how undesirable it may be; but the refining of the undesirable into the constructive and elevating; the lifting of the lower into the higher.

A hell of fire and brimstone finds no place in the category of the Christic Interpretation. Generally understood, it is a place wherein man is punished for things done which should have been left undone; or for the sins of omission. That man is punished *for* his sins either here or in the future is an erroneous idea; he is punished *by* his sins, either now or sometime in the future, and this is what is meant by "thy sins have found thee out." Of all the punishment inflicted on man, that of fear is the most terrible; and all who labor under it are in hell, a hades as surely as would be one composed of fire and brimstone. How few have been free from the awful suffering caused by waiting for a calamity which is expected; the fear, the suspense, the dread, and the uncertainty—that is hell. Sitting and waiting, constantly expecting, dreading to make a move, thinking faculties paralyzed, reasoning power in abeyance, sense restricted to breath, this is hell, destructive to soul and body.

Man must become the master; these conditions must be changed, and can be by an understanding of the promise made to him by the Divine Will, which must be accepted with trust, and a manifesting of the faith in them by living accordingly. Man must think, act, and regulate his actions in harmony with the dictates of the Law and he will gain liberty from all that is undesirable, thereby gaining power, and making Health certain.

Fear cannot be mastered by mere faith in the promises of the All Father; but can be overcome only through thoughts and actions that harmonize with the Law whereon the promises rest. All undesirable passions and emotions relax their grasp only as we manifest faith in the Divine Law by regulating our every day existence in harmony with it; and thus we grow into love, wisdom, and true understanding; and in exact proportion as we develop these within us will fear vanish. "Perfect love casteth out fear."

Life throughout is a growth; likewise is all true knowledge. Mere belief in the truth of a statement does not constitute understanding. Acceptance of the teachings of another will not pass as wisdom. Enlightenment is that which we feel within ourselves; realizing it is a part of our very life, manifesting through our inner consciousness; and the more we live in harmony with the Divine Law, the greater will be the wisdom we shall obtain.

Wisdom is like a mustard seed; accept a little of it and live accordingly, and it will gain greatly, and deliver you from the bondage of ignorance. Fear is the outgrowth, the legitimate fruit of ignorance and error. Courage, faith, and hope are the children of knowledge and love. All conditions under which man suffers have a work to perform, a mission to fulfill, a purpose to satisfy; through them man is induced to seek for wisdom. Without pain and sorrow, man would make no effort to gain freedom; without knowing fear man could not understand peace of mind and the joys of love; without knowledge of hate, he could not realize the power of friendship and forgiveness; and without experiencing the absence of love, little or nothing would be known of the potency and efficacy of it. Thus with all the passions and vices and sorrows; man must experience them all in order to desire their opposite; and the only reason for evil is to enable one to choose the good. This is not an indication that man should indulge in evil for the sake of appreciating the constructive, nor that he should deliberately experience wrong and error, sin and suffering, to gain knowledge of the value of their opposite.

The duty of man, now that he is on the earth plane, is to transmute all undesirable passions and emotions, no matter what they may be, into that which gives greater strength, power, and efficiency. This is true whether it concerns hate, anger, malice, ill-will, or destructive habits which have become a part of our nature. They must all be changed into health, strength, harmony, wisdom, happiness; and finally and ultimately, into Conscious Individuality,—immortality of soul.

All that we now consider a task, duty, or even a yoke, and which we bow under because we think we must, must be transformed from a chain of bondage into a garland of flowers—of love, a privilege which will help us toward realization.

Man must be wedded (bound) to something; otherwise he would stand alone and separate from all; but his is the choice of the bond. He may choose that which results from fear, ultimately leading to death; or love and all that belongs to the divine passion, gradually leading him toward Light, and Life, and Immortality.

The inception of real life—of strength, health, power, Individuality and Sonship, is at the moment man accepts the glorious truth that he is created in the image of the Father; that he possesses in himself all power, all potentialities, all that is in God, the first Creator, though in lesser degree; in fact, the truth that he *is* the temple of the living God. This recognition is merely the beginning; the point from whence the start is to be made; once having accepted this truth, he must, like the builder of temples and mansions, follow the art of building from the very foundation until the structure is finished. He must be most careful in the material he accepts; must know how to direct the work, and how to continue faithfully until the building is complete and beautiful in its perfection. This we teach.

Accepting the first truth, the foundation principle, and building according to his understanding of the truth, man will also begin to comprehend what it means to have freedom, not merely from the bondage of fear, but from all that stultify his forces through it. As he commences to actually live, he will grow; as he grows he will manifest the fruits, always the result of obedience to Nature's Laws.

Man was not created to be the victim of fear; nor to suffer; surely not to die. He was to be free, fearless as his Creator. He is to enjoy life, and to know happiness. Made in the image of the Father, he is to live forever; and so shall he live when he has learned to sever the bonds that bind him; when he has thrown aside the limitations resultant on race beliefs which have been his mortal enemies, lo, these many centuries.

The Soul seed (the Divine Spark) that is now in man could not gain knowledge without the body, the flesh is of the earth and with its limitations; consequently, through its own volition, it "fell" into matter and the shortcomings thereof. It is impossible for the soul to again know God and become like Him, returning to its ideal state through retaining the knowledge it has gathered during the pilgrimage, without accepting the great truth that the present life is for the purpose of obtaining wisdom and enlightenment, and more especially for the redeeming of the soul from all undesirable conditions. The soul reclaims itself, *not* through some special favor granted it by God, or because of the intercession of one called Jesus, *but through its own efforts, its own worthiness, its desires and volition,* harmonizing with the instructions given man by Jesus and other great teachers.

Redemption, full, complete, and perfect, has reference not alone to the soul, but to the body, and signifies freedom of body and soul. The physical being shall become purified from the elements that bind the carnal to it; shall become partner and co-worker with the soul, sharing its pleasures, its joys, and its harmonious states which the soul can alone enjoy.

To what paramount desire in man can we point above all others to prove that death was not planned by the Divine Will as the goal for man? What longing, greater than any, sways most men, and is strongest in them? Search the hearts of men, seek for the most hidden desire, not merely for the one they seemingly think is in the ascendant, but the actual, possibly unconscious aspiration. There are many, numberless indeed, who, being ill, long for health; others, multitudes, who, loveless, seek affection; hordes, who, without possession, wish for riches; but these are not the *living* desires in the universal human heart. It is *life, a fulness of being,* that rules the inmost heart of humanity.

According to all the masters of the past, the philosophers of all ages, it is *actually* possible for man to attain that which the heart actively longs for, provided he is willing to put forth the effort, to accept the self-denial and the struggle necessary to attainment. This being admitted, who is there to deny that the desire for life, being the strongest and most universal, is capable of fulfillment? Especially may we grant the possibility when we are aware that every true teacher and philosopher, including Jesus, promised the redemption of both body and soul.

Eternal life will not be achieved through a knowledge of eugenics and race improvement; nor will it be possible through the perfection of body only; it is only when men comprehend that it is essential to refine and regenerate *both* body and soul at the same time; the building into the soul the desire for continual life. This must charge every cell, every atom, in the entire body, and vitalize the entire being, with both physical and spiritual energy.

This *can* be accomplished; it is merely necessary for the human family to accept the promise, and to live according to the instructions given. *Think of life;* but, aside from the thought, *live in harmony with it.* Charge every cell of your body, not with fear, as in the past, but with freedom; not with hate, but with love; not with grudges and ill-will, but with forgiveness; not with envy of the possessions of others, but with blessings to them, and a sincere wish that they may have happiness and a fuller life; and with a longing that you may yourself gain all that is essential to your happiness and well-being.

Life cannot be divided into degrees; it is through the living we gain results, irrespective of the doctrine we accept. If we live according to the laws of death, we shall reap the fruits; if we guide ourselves in harmony with the dictates of Nature, God grants us a fuller life. Ours is the choice; success and health is ours for the asking.

Awakening

Some of the organized churches are beginning to see the danger in the enactment of so-called "Blue Laws;" the Adventists declaring that Congressional encroachment in the Spiritual realm would enforce hypocrisy by law. Such a conclusion is unquestionably correct.

Washington, Jan. 15.—Sunday Blue Laws are described as encroachment of civil power into the spiritual realm, in a memorial adopted by the General Conference Committee of Seventh-Day Adventists made public to-day at headquarters here. Opposition to all Sunday laws is declared, particularly to proposed Federal enactments.

"Asserting that the complete separation of church and state was essential to the country's well-being, the memorial declares that failure to recognize this distinction in the past had been the primary cause of religious persecutions. The present *strong organized effort* to secure Blue Law enactments, it added, are destructive both to the church and the state, however innocent they may appear, *and if successful will eventually destroy the pillars upon which our government is founded.*

"Sabbath-keeping is not a civil but a religious duty, the memorial declared. Congress therefore has nothing whatever to do with the question of its observance.

"Only those whose hearts God has changed can truly keep a holy Sabbath. As no legislation by Congress can change the human heart, to make citizens perform a religious act when they are not religious *is to enforce hypocrisy by law.*

"Honest labor is no more uncivil on Sunday than on Monday. It is only religious prejudices which are disturbed by labor on this day more than on other days. But bolstering up some particular theological dogma and protecting the religious prejudices of citizens is not the business of congress."—*The Philadelphia Inquirer, Sunday January 16, 1921.*

Chapter Thirteen

The Life of Sin Alone Brings Death.

What is sin? This question depends all on having refer-ence to the higher life.

Not merely is sin all that affects the soul and gives it status in the life beyond death, but it is all-inclusive of everything having influence on man here and now. Sin has been considered as the committance of deeds which deny entrance into the realm of bliss in the Hereafter; acts of daily life, possibly of hourly indulgences; the only direct effect of which is to prevent man's entrance into a sphere of delight, joy and peace; thoughts, de-sires, and acts which are contrary to the will of God. While it is true that all these make their impression on the soul, and concern its relation with God, by no means does it end there; on the contrary, they powerfully retard or elevate the person-ality and individuality, having a bearing on health, strength and efficiency, as well as the peace and satisfaction, and the harmony of life *here and now.*

' The New Commandment maintains and inculcates as an absolute fact that any thought, desire, or act, irrespective of its nature, is a sin if in any manner it is injurious either to the participant or to any other; and, further, that it is not merely an article of faith but an actual truth founded on common sense and reason, that any thought, desire, or act which is harm-ful to neither the participant and does not visit suffering and sorrow to another cannot be wrong nor sin. There is not the slightest difference between that termed a sin and what others designate wrong-doing, wrong-living, or working against the best interests of others; in principle they are the same. For instance, hygienic law is on an equality with moral and ethical law; care of the body is as important as regard for the soul; habits which influence the welfare of the physical being, whether respecting food and drink, or any other factor of health and efficiency, to be classed as injurious or noninjurious, and, consequently, as right or wrong, constructive or sinful. To indulge in eating or drinking that which is harmful to the physical being is not only destructive to the person, but is actually committing a sin, one that directly affects the soul. Sin is any death dealing agency, any destructive principle, all harmful and injurious habits. To be guilty of living out of harmony with Nature's Law, thus bringing hurt to the physical being, is living a sinful, death-dealing life.

In the earth life the body is as important as the soul; otherwise God were to be condemned for having influenced man to accept it. To entertain happy, wholesome, generous thoughts is not all of righteousness as some seem to think, who are hypnotized by unreasoning philosophies and forgetful of logic. The thoughts and desires of an individual may be free from carnality and every form of selfishness, jealousy, ill-will, envy; his life may appear to be a model one; but if he devotes his entire attention to business or to the work in hand, if he denies the physical man the attention it requires; if he refuses to allow sufficient time for sleep and rest, and does not provide correct food, permitting the body to be nourished and rebuilt, it is a certainty he is guilty of violating physical, therefore Nature's laws and consequently guilty of sin and error, as truly as if he had deliberately defied moral law.

God is a *just* God, which indicates He balances all things; because only in balance, the perfect equilibrium of all things, is there justice; that the Law of Hermes, "As above, so Below," logically proves the body is no less important than the soul, nor the soul greater than the body; the soul's greatness actually depending largely on the rejuvenation and regeneration, and the purity of the body; nor can a well-developed and enlightened soul dwell in an unclean (physically and morally) body.

Manifestedly it is natural to conclude that a wrong life is truly a sinful one; the sinful life in turn the one that results in disease, sorrow, suffering, and, ultimately, an ignoble death; one never intended by the Creator, but become necessary only as man gave up the exalted life and accepted the race belief in the impossibility of maintaining life continually, thus charging and magnetizing every cell of the body with the thoughts of weakness, sickness, and death.

God created man in His own image; that is, He Himself is sinless and eternal, knowing not death; and in His likeness He moulded man. But with this heritage He gave man free-will, a faculty he still possesses. God, being perfect, harbors only ideals; and these He conferred upon the soul of man. Man was not satisfied with perfection in its simplicity; consequently, he used his power, or gift, of free-will for ignoble purposes; and through this misuse gradually fell into the conditions, desires, and beliefs, which made death a necessity. Having been created perfect, man should be sinless, consequently deathless.

The New Commandment maintains as a fundamental truth that man may gradually and naturally find the path leading to a sinless, sorrowless, deathless life; but to do this, he must inaugurate two important changes. First, he must purify his thoughts, desires, and beliefs; entertaining only those which harmonize with the doctrine of a life free from illness, sorrow, and failure. Second, he must change his life and conduct to coincide with the transmutation of thought, desire, and belief. He must commence living the natural life, supplying the body with food and drink, recreation and rest it requires and which God had intended it should have; this will be making Health certain.

It is essential he cease making business the supreme God that claims all his thoughts, desires, and time. He must commence to live for the sake of life itself, not merely because he seeks to be successful in business and advance beyond the status of his competitors; must cease to sacrifice pleasures, friends, family, and, last and greatest, his soul and God for business, as the multitudes are doing. It is necessary to give each and all of these interests part of his time, as much as the Divine and Natural Law demands for his welfare. There are many who claim this to be impossible; but proofs are always before us that man *must*, sooner or later, satisfy the Law in this respect; if he refuses to comply willingly, the Great Fiat demands it by denuding him of success, business, and possessions, through sickness, suffering, or other misfortune, and, finally, an immature death.

Naturally, the question arises, What is man willing to do? Is he willing to apportion his time judiciously among the varied interests that should have his attention; to meet the normal demands of his nature for development of body, recreation and pleasure? Is he ready to satisfy the demands of his soul and the voice of God speaking through it; to live the natural, normal life, free from disease and suffering, achieving success on every plane of being? Or does he prefer the strenuous life; having neither time nor inclination for physical development, temple-building, or natural pleasures; for home, friends, and God; giving time only to business and zealous competition?

The same law governing man also applies to woman. With women generally, it is slavery of another kind; not thraldom under business demands, but a serfdom to unnecessary home cares, dress, society, and hundreds of other concerns which appear necessary to womankind, but both unnatural and abnormal. The interests to which woman becomes a slave she herself admits are not sources of real happiness; she allows them to rule her in the same spirit in which man cares for his business; because competitors are to be outdistanced.

Such subjects as these are not usually supposed to have any connection with a philosophy dealing with the soul and man's relation with God. They are, nevertheless, the foundation of serfdom or freedom from disease and suffering, sorrow and unhappiness; of a long and useful life, soul development, and illumination; and, finally, of the attainment of success and happiness. Upon enlightenment must the temple structure be erected; if the fundamentals are unsound, the whole edifice will be insecure and unable to bear the test of time.

Man is created in the image of the Father; within him is the nucleus for perfection of body, soul, and all that is lasting. Although this likeness to the Perfect Being is only in embryo, it is none the less a veritable possibility of being brought into manifestation. This being true, why should man be sinful? Why guilty of that which is conducive neither to perfection of body nor development of mind and soul? Despite the reward offered, it is freely admitted practically all men are living and thinking contrary to the Law of Conscious Evolution as respecting, body, mind, and soul.

Universally considered, man is a carnal, sinful being, a creature given to wrong thinking and acting, one who generally sets aside both Natural and Divine Law; *not* because he was accursed through the acts of our first parents, but by reason of a race belief which induces him to think that such an existence is easiest and requires least effort. Because of this he undergoes punishment; blame cannot be placed on God the Father; his own thoughts and acts are responsible for setting into motion forces which bring about this just chastisement. When sickness, sorrow, and finally death stalk before man, he holds God guilty; he blames Nature; accuses everyone but himself for his imbecility and weakness; when in truth, no one is at fault but himself. Men must come to a clear understanding that it is *not* God who punishes, but the thoughts, desires, and acts, *rebounding upon ourselves through the forces we set in motion.* A homely old saying known to us all, clearly expresses the Law: "Chickens come home to roost." Jesus expressed this in more refined language when he said: "As ye sow so shall ye reap," while the ancient Philosophers and teachers voiced the same truth in the Law of Karma.

Enough has been taught concerning the Divine and Natural law that man can on longer plead ignorance respecting them. Though many elevating doctrines have been given false representation and beclouded interpretations, nevertheless, if man actually lived according to the light he does possess, his condition would be far better than it is. Even obedience to prevalent teachings merely because he thought they concerned the soul in its future state would be of real benefit to him in making Health possible.

We are living in an age wherein man must come to a clear comprehension that religion embraces not only all that is of welfare to the soul, but that *it is the law of God and governing every department of his nature.* Or, if one disbelieves in God, let him understand distinctly that religion is *the law of nature,* dealing primarily with the well-being of the body and with all that really concerns life in its first application to man; let him know that in proportion as religion such as here inculcated is applied to the every day life on the material plane, will it effect the soul.

Religion will shortly come to be understood as the Law of Life. Life in this sense referring to existence as it is from the moment that the Divine Spark leaves the heavenly sphere, down through its birth, onward through existence on this plane, until man enters Immortality. It is immaterial where life will continue, whether on the present plane or in the Beyond of the soul realm. True religion is the Law of life, inclusive of all that concerns man on *every* plane of existence.

God is not sinful; nor sorrowful, nor yet dying; He is life, Light, Love, Wisdom, Happiness, is all of Eternity. Man is created in this image of Light, Love, Happiness and Eternal Life, and this is firmly impressed upon his heart though covered with the rubbish of degrading desires. He is heir to all of these; but can enter upon his inheritance only as he complies with the dictates of the Divine Will which has existed since the very beginning of time. If he refuses to obey the terms of the Infinite in the true spirit rather than according to the letter, he cannot benefit by the blessings the Divine Will would confer upon him: Thus, God being an eternal reality, free from all that is undesirable, man likewise may be greater than such conditions if he be willing to live as the normal, natural, divine man should.

As man is at the moment, he may conclude this to mean self-denial and the exclusion of all that which seemingly makes life worth living; this is an entirely false conclusion; true religion does not deny man anything really good and constructive; it permits him every honest, wholesome recreation; desirable social intercourse, and encourages interest in honest business or the professions. Music, flowers, and the beauties of nature and art should be part of his life; refuses him only such pleasures as are certain to visit illness and weakness, sorrow and failure, upon him.

The New Commandment encourages all that is for the well-being of man; teaching only that which will ultimately produce a perfect being, one having true faith and living accordingly. This is the Way to life, making Health certain.

Chapter Fourteen

Healing of the Sick

All who have learned the divine truth, either through experience or special training, receive a two-fold command from God. First, they are to teach the truth to the multitudes who are ignorant and unenlightened. Second, they are to heed the divine command, "Heal the sick." Consequently, those who fulfill their entire duty must teach and heal all who come to them in faith and with the desire to obey.

In this department of the Great Work—teaching the truth and healing the ailing—practically very little can be accomplished unless the teacher-healer command faith in the possibility of healing; this is neither unnatural nor unreasonable. History, indicates that all the teacher-healers of the past, including Jesus, demanded faith on the part of those who sought help; unless the supplicant professed full confidence, he could not be relieved of his infirmity. This is not an arbitrary demand on the part of those who offer their services; it is merely a necessary condition for obtaining relief; and is a state of mind making it possible for the sufferer to receive or to appropriate healing influences. In this sense only, is faith essential; and the law of healing is expressed in the oft-repeated saying of Jesus, "According to thy faith be it unto thee."

In bringing relief to the sick something more is required on the part of the healer than the use of some healing power; it is necessary for him to teach the Natural and Divine Law, the natural life, to all who come to him. Unless he does this, though he might heal some for a time, the disease, not being eradicated, but merely held in suspension, would return; because that which caused the disease in the first place will bring about a recurrence.

The New Commandment maintains as an absolute fact, that an unnatural life, incorrect food and drink, lack of sleep, exercise and recreation, and unemployment of mind and body, *is a sin;* a violation of the divine and natural law. He who commits error will be afflicted sooner or later with some disease, despite all the healers in the world, and any faith, however strong, he might possess. Were this untrue, then God's Law would favor the few at the expense of the many and would be unjust, therefore satanic. God does not merely desire a man to have faith in His goodness, but requires him to be in harmony with his expressed confidence by ordaining his life in harmony with the faith.

We confess that the sufferer's faith in the healer and the power of God manifesting through him, might be great enough that the disease afflicting the body for many years would fall away as though it had never existed; but if the life thereafter is not in harmony with Nature's law the body cannot long remain free from disease and its consequent suffering.

Illness is in reality a sin, or the result of sin; this is amply indicated in the sayings of Jesus. In some instances he said, "Be thou whole (holy)" which is the same as to command, "Be thou free from disease." To others, he said, "Thy sins be forgiven thee." Yet again, "Go thy way and sin no more." This indicated a concern for the future of the one healed; clearly and undeniably threatening a recurrence of the disease were the person to defy God's law, and sin—commit error. Consequently, we inculcate the doctrine that the chief duty of the healer is to teach those whom he relieves, the natural laws of life, a normal system of living, and the Way to Life. It is actually more important for man to understand how to be free from sin, disease, and suffering, than to be made whole when ill.

The mission of the teacher-healer is more extensive than this; not only should he minister to the body, helping to free it from its burden of pain and suffering, but the heart of the weary should be relieved and made joyous. The soul free from sin has no sorrow; it understands the reason for all that comes its way; even the loss of a friend dearly beloved does not bring the pain and the anguish that come to those living in sin. Such a soul comprehends that death is merely a transition, that "passing away" is but temporary and for the greater welfare of the one entering the "great experience."

Why should faith on the part of the sufferer be essential if God is all-inclusive? Why is it not possible for the teacher-healer to be able to charge and magnetize the body of the afflicted with such intense vibrations as to free it from illness despite a lack of faith?

Let it be clearly understood that the Law ever has been, and ever will be: Any substance, whatever its nature, is unable to receive unless it has previously been prepared. As an illustration: In the making of a magnet it is not every material that will receive the charge of electricity and retain part of it, through this detention becoming a magnet. Only certain substances, after careful preparation, will be magnets after being charged. *All things are under this same natural law.* The body of the sick is governed thereby; and though charge after charge of healing energy might be transfused through the diseased body, health will not be restored to it unless it has been prepared to receive and retain the healing influence. Faith, in this instance, is the agency that prepares the body to receive and retain the constructive force. If the afflicted one has not the desire to receive, and the confidence requisite, he is as the metal bar unprepared for the electric charge. Though the current were to be sent through it, in place of being retained, it would pass on, merely a flight in the air, having accomplished no good.

The greater man's faith, the more desirable the results achieved. If strong and unwavering in the healing influence, then on being received it will so charge and magnetize every cell of the body with a living fire that the vibrations of health, being higher and more intense than those of disease, will actually burn out such condition and influence every atom of the body for health. The one in sin, will be made whole (holy). "Thy sins be forgiven thee." Such is the promise that makes Health certain.

From the above it will readily be comprehended that the Law *is*, "According to thy faith, so shall it be unto thee." There is no power on earth, nor in heaven; none under the earth or in the sea, which can successfully and permanently heal the afflicted body and mind if there is not: First, a keen desire for health and harmony. Second, a willingness to obey Nature's law. Third, Faith in the possibility of the accomplishment. If there is such a desire, meekness and faith, then will the sufferer receive the forces and energies as they flow from the fountain of life, from the Godhead, the Great Storehouse of Light and Life, and be able to retain these vivifying agencies, thus making Health possible.

The old theory that it is God, or the Lord, or Jesus, who performs the miracles is denied emphatically by the Christic Interpretation.   Assuredly, the forces and energies come from God; but He is not the healer in an arbitrary sense any more than He is the one who commits the sins and errors causing the diseases.   Man, thinking destructively, and living the laws of death, rather than of life, brings disease and suffering and sorrow upon himself.   In like manner, through the awakening of his God-given faculties, thinking constructively, and living naturally, with a keen faith in the possibility of health and power, he may draw to himself and retain the vibrations and forces that will quickly overcome weakness and inefficiency, cast aside sorrow and debasement, and be restored to health.   Admittedly the healing belongs to God, being good, but it is by no means correct to state that He gives it to man; rather does God permit us to receive and use it as we will.   Man is not a slave; he is free and unlimited in his potencies; not the supplicator, but the partaker with God.

As many times stated, God made man in His own image; He has also created a storehouse of life, force, energy, and power; to man He gave the Key to this Treasurehouse; and this he may employ to open the door as his needs require.   The Key is Faith and a desire for greater life.   He who has faith and is willing to live, will be enabled to draw from this Treasury as much as he can rightly use; and the Law is such that, the more he uses the greater the supply he may draw therefrom.   God neither gives, nor does He refuse; man is free to accept all he requires to meet with success, and to make Health certain.

Certain conditions are connected with the acceptance and employing of these powers and energies.   The first of these, as previously mentioned, is faith. The second, that man shall live in accordance with his belief. If he fails to meet these several requirements, he loses the Key to the Depository of power and energy, and cannot draw therefrom. God forces no man to accept, but offers to everyone the privilege. If we ourselves lose the key, and the power to draw ourselves when in need, it will often be necessary for some one to act as intermediary, as an agent between us and the Source of Force and Energy; it is then we require the service of the true teacher-healer; and it was such service Jesus and others offered mankind, teaching many to "teach and to heal."

Man's sickness and suffering is not a punishment from God visited upon disobedient mankind; nor does he send sorrow, misery, or misfortune to any one; on the contrary, man through his own thoughts and deeds draws upon himself the conditions befalling him. *The law operates like a two-edged sword.* Just as he draws upon himself undesirable conditions, as disease, suffering, and misfortune through his destructive thoughts and mode of living, in like manner may he be blessed with all that is desirable, as Life, Light, Love, and Immortality. Instead of thinking, desiring, and living the life that ends in death, he may choose to think, long for, and so order his life that all Eternity is offered him, and "all things are added unto him." Through this conversion of thought, feeling, and action, he attracts to himself Life, Light, and Love, in place of disease, sorrow and weakness. God gives neither one nor the other; he graciously permits man to choose and accept; he denies man nothing, neither the good nor the ill; but grants him the privilege to do as he pleases and to accept the reward or the penalty, according to the desire and the act.

Truly may it be stated, it is not God who restores the sick and the suffering; but living according to our faith—this restores to health those sick and suffering. God does not take life as so often acclaimed; He does not set the time of death; nor does He number the days of man's life. He offers life continuously, teaches man how to live through imitation of Nature's methods; clearly indicating that to all who fully obey shall endure neither sickness or eternal death. On the contrary, He gives man no reason whatever to lead him to believe that He, God the Father, will overcome death for him; but unmistakably indicates that man *must overcome death for himself*. This he must do through faith in the promise, and obedience to the Law, this is making Health certain.

For ages man believed that redemption, salvation, or immortality, call it by what appellation you wish, did not concern the body; that it was immaterial how pain-racked the body might be, how diseased, or how awful its suffering, if he had faith in salvation, that at death the soul would fly to heaven, he would be "redeemed through the blood of Jesus." That age is at an end; men now know, even those who do not believe in constituted religion, that redemption is not of the soul alone, but concerns the body equally; that the body is actually the reflection of its spiritual counterpart; know that when inner Illumination and enlightenment has been attained, the soul will illumine the outer covering, or body. They know that as is the God within, so will become the body without; and, in like manner, as is the body, so will become the soul.

We dare not overlook the fact that the body may be perfect in outward appearance, may be healthy and strong, yet destitute of goodness and spirituality; for there are animal natures in the form of man wherein is neither kindness nor soulfulness. These can scarcely be classed as human beings; they are more like unto healthy and well cared for animals, possessing the instincts and appetites of these and other exploiters of the innocent, or pawns in the hands of the strong; they come and they pass, and are no more.

But, argues the critic, how can this be consistent with the teachings that every thought, desire, and act, makes an impression upon the body and produces corresponding effects?

Unquestionably every desire, thought, and deed leaves its impress of their character upon the body and affect it accordingly. This is an absolute Law; but there is another equally as great, one not generally known or understood. To illustrate: a dog may be perfect in every respect, as a dog, yet be possessed of a vicious temper, one making him dangerous, and unsafe to be free lest he injure those who may come near him; this disposition of the dog does not shorten its life, does not interfere with the digestion of its food, nor impair its health. Why not? Because it is the nature of the dog, and he lives according to his nature. Had the dog a soul, that something within which confers to him the right and power of choice, then viciousness would act as a poison to his system and result in disease and suffering. The dog has no soul, is born, lives his life, and dies as just what he is, a vicious dog.

Undesirable as it may seem, there are humans born in the nature of such dogs; through some cause, but always of their own choice at one time or another, they have destroyed the individuality within; and no longer possess that divine monitor, called the Divine Spark, which places upon them the responsibility of their acts. They merely exist according to their nature; and within them there is nothing to either receive or to reflect their thoughts and deeds, consequently, malicious thoughts, destructive desires, and degrading acts do not arouse a poisonous condition to disturb normal bodily functions; thus, they, like the animal, are born, live their lives, and die, according to nature.

This illustration prepares for a statement and a consideration of the Law. Man is body, mind, and spirit; and within the three there is that which we term the "Divine Spark," or the soul. This nucleus, being of God and constituting man different from the animal, is the *receiver* and *storehouse* of impressions. *It is also a reflector.* All that the divine entity receives it will reflect; and this is shown in the body of man, for it is the temple of God, as of the soul. In those beings in whom there is no such Divine Spark, where there is no reflector, as like with animals, even though the nature is renegade, it is not reflected in the personality and the body, except possibly in certain cases to make it more nearly perfect; the animal creation always tending towards physical perfection.

This interpretation may seem harsh; but is in perfect harmony with God's teachings as well as with those of all the philosophers of the past, and in absolute concord with Nature's laws. Nature recognizes no soul in her creation; nevertheless, her manifestations are perfect. Man alone, possessing free-will and the Spark of Divinity, reflects in his character his desires, thoughts, and deeds. The animal, on the contrary, being the product of Nature *alone*, always manifests toward physical perfection because she herself is so, though changeable and never individualized in entities that continue permanently.

Superman

Man was not created to be the victim of fear; nor to suffer; surely not to die. He was to be free, fearless as his Creator. He is to enjoy life, and to know happiness. Made in the image of the Father, he is to live forever; and so shall he live when he has learned to sever the bonds that bind him; when he has thrown aside the limitations resultant on race beliefs which have been his mortal enemies, lo, these many centuries.

The duty of man, now that he is on the earth plane, is to transmute all undesirable passions and emotions, no matter what they may be, into that which gives greater strength, power, and efficiency. This is true whether it concerns hate, anger, malice, ill-will, or destructive habits which have become a part of our nature. They must all be changed into health, strength, harmony, wisdom, happiness; and finally and ultimately, into Conscious Individuality,—immortality of soul.

Chapter Eleven

Why be Sick

Why should man be sick? Correctly speaking, why should he be living a sinful life?

There is no logical reason inducing man not to live in conformity with higher ideals, thereby reaping the benefit resultant of being in harmony with eternal laws.

Sin and sickness are actually one and the same; one resulting from the other. Sin is synonymous with incorrect living and wrong doing; is the result of ignorance, producing death as the final penalty.

Sin is classed as such because it is the opposite of good; not for the reason that God is supposed to have said man should not do thus and so; nor because theology outlines it as such; or that philosophers have said that to do certain things is to commit wrong; but from the indisputable fact it brings pain and sorrow, loss and misery, harm and injury, either to the one who commits it or to those against whom acted. There is *no other basis from which to judge what is sin.* Why should sensible man be guilty of misdeeds and self-destruction, but for the one reason that he labors under the mistaken idea regarding life and conduct; one that has become a race belief, consequently a part of his inner nature,—he believes that to be active along certain lines will be to his advantage, bringing him profit, pleasure, and honor.

There are actually very few men who are guilty of error or

deliberate misdoing because of a love for the wrong. Admittedly there are such; human nature being capable of perversion. These we term degenerates; reasoning that anyone who loves to do that which is contrary to natural and divine law must have fallen below man's true estate. The renegade delights in doing that which is contrary to the laws of Nature and of God; takes pleasure in indulgences at which nature revolts; but this class is in the minority, though steadily increasing in number. The vast majority of mankind delight in the right; committing evil only through the mistaken idea that what they do is the only method whereby they may obtain all desirable possessions.

The performance of all which the mind and heart recognize as wrong and not in harmony with the Law, even when with superficial thought and indifferent purpose, leaves its mark upon the body of the actor, results in weakness, sickness, failure and ultimately in death.

Few indeed, who are not aware that a fit of anger is wrong, that it is actually of no benefit, and cannot right a wrong; humanity in general is conversant with experiments having been made, proving that it creates a poison destructive both to mind and body. Despite this knowledge, how very few make any great effort to control it? This constitutes sin; knowing that it is wrong, not by reason of the passion itself, but because it creates that something which is destructive, and giving it countenance in one's life.

By becoming angry, man liberates a poison in his organism; this causes a disturbed condition and induces illness; by virtue of this creation of something which is destructive to the self, anger is constituted a sin and to be avoided.

All of us have been admonished against the evil of

selfishness, yet how few have been able to tear it from the heart? One might reasonably question if many have even attempted to do so. Conservatively speaking, possibly more than one-fifth of all illness has its base in selfishness. As these lines are being penned we have domiciled at the Hall a patient suffering from a severe case of Arthritis; developed to a degree resulting in deformation of various joints, the patient having suffered for more than ten years and consulted the world's most famous specialists. Careful examination and watchfulness of thoughts, desires, and actions, clearly indicate, nay, actually proves, the basic cause to be a poison constantly created by inner selfishness so deeply rooted that there is no thought but of the self and even appetite and pleasure is considered rather than a willingness to refrain from a few things which would help to bring about relief.

Indisputably all the great passions, as, hate, malice, resentment, and jealousy are destructive and self-poisoning in their character; therefore, must be classed as sinful. It is the same with the minor emotions; those springing from the greater, and often these are so thoroughly covered as to be unrecognizable; nevertheless, just as destructive in their ultimate results.

What is to be the remedy for the eradication of these sins, these destructive forces? The answer is plain and easily understood: Love, Compassion, and Forgiveness.

These are the divine attributes, the cardinal virtues; with them we may ultimately destroy all gross and destroying evils. As man truly develops, he will transmute the degenerating forces into creative energies; making of them constructive potentialities, thereby assuring health and success.

But, argues the self, why should I love those who attempt

to destroy my happiness; who sin against me; whose aim is to ruin me, and defame me?

Why should you "hate them that spitefully use you?" Do you imagine that this will change them; that it will induce them to cease their machinations? Can you imagine your hatred will do them any harm, or be beneficial to yourself? Disabuse your mind of such an idea. Seldom will your hatred reach them or serve as a punishment; while it may stimulate, intensify and exaggerate their undesirable actions toward yourself, "like attracting like."

Contrariwise, if you will change your hatred into forgiveness, the beneficial results to yourself will be quickly noticed, enabling you to overcome every obstacle that may be placed in your path; and your love and good-will toward your enemies will act as an attracting power, drawing whatever good is in them. Moreover, your own resentment changed into love acts as a vivifying agency within yourself; and, instead of inducing illness and mental depression, with its sorrows, will give you health, love, and life. Whereas hatred and resentment arouse poisonous conditions resulting in disease and illness, forgiveness and compassion are health-inspiring tonics that promote poise, peace, and tranquility of body and mind. Admittedly, it may require a mighty effort to offer love and compassion in exchange for grudges, losses, and malice; but the reward is proportionate to the effort, the gain is worth the price, though it should not be understood the New Commandment advocates the wronged to seek for those who sin against them and offer their solicitations like abject slaves; forgiveness is in the heart and need not be outwardly displayed.

By transmuting the destructive emotions into life-giving,

constructive forces, they return to us for good manifold. When men comprehend this truth they will honor the Law of Transmutation, enabling them to transmute all the dross of error and sin into the pure gold of love, forgiveness, and kindly-feeling; and as men come to realize that degrading passions can accomplish good to none; that by indulging one can not change the plans or the feelings of others, they will arouse every effort to free themselves from this type of sin; this will be making Health certain.

Respecting the statement that sin is the cause of sickness, whether committed by us or others, it is freely admitted that indulgence may be innocent in so far as the desire to do wrong is concerned. Nevertheless, all wrong, and every act that is not in harmony with natural or divine law, constitutes sin and itself sets into motion forces which return the legitimate penalty according to its nature. "Ignorance of the law excuses none," and it behooves each one to understand the Law. The sooner we learn all the requirements of a natural, normal life, the shorter will be the time for us to remain in bondage to the undesirable in life; and chief among the rewards will be freedom from sickness, sorrow, and failure.

The first object of life should be seeking an avenue to escape from ignorance and error; an understanding of the Law; becoming accurate in discrimination for the sake of choosing all that is constructive, upbuilding, and life-giving, and rejecting the things that are destructive to life and all dear to it. Having learned this, it remains for us to live according to the constructive principles whereby we may be continually improving the temple of life; increasing the resisting, energizing forces within us. This pertains not only to the body, but likewise to the soul. Life of the body alone is animal life; life of body and soul is divine; and none can be truly human or god-like unless he honors body and soul alike, regarding one equal in importance with the other.

Jesus called this the "holy (whole) life." Living thus, honoring divine and natural law in the daily routine, ultimately attaining Illumination of Soul; this is termed "receiving the Holy Ghost.' When we cleanse the body and free it from sin and sickness; and the soul from its grave of earth; then will we reach Realization, and attain the greater life, entering here and now, into the kingdom of heaven.

The New Commandment inculcates the doctrine that the beginning of this holy life must be in faith. Unless the one desiring the benefits is willing to so live as to earn them, and in full confidence that he will receive them, there can be no results. It emphasizes the fact that, when man once awakens to these great truths, comprehending it to be to his benefit to arrange his life in harmony with the law, then his faith, if sufficiently strong, will induce him to follow the dictates of the exalted mind here indicated. Having made a beginning, he will eventually become firmly established in faith and life, and the results will quickly become manifest.

Thereafter he will no longer need to live by faith alone; but through knowledge of power. It is knowledge undeniably because he realizes results which can come only through obedience. Gradually, the holy (whole) life becomes his natural, normal mode of existence, bringing him into consciousness of the Godhead and of his own Individuality.

Likewise with the sick and afflicted. In the beginning it is faith, with some degree of self-effort. He must commence to educate and train his thoughts, and desires, and to conform his conduct in harmony with the natural and divine law; then the new life, through the creation of energies and powers heretofore unknown, will free him from disease and suffering; will lead him toward Realization; the life without sin, conscious and eternal.

We are not to think of God as the One who possesses power to liberate us from sickness and failure; rather, as the One who has made us in His own image; endowing man with power to gain his freedom from sin; and to sever the bonds which bind us to error and ignorance. God is all power—this we admit; but He does not use it to help us; He delegates to us the *right and privilege* of employing it to manifest the Godhood within ourselves, thus making Health certain.

"As above, so below," is the Law, and we should reason by comparison. It is as if our earthly parents, having abundant possession, should give us *carte blanche* to draw upon their resources. We have a perfect right to draw upon God's great storehouse to the full extent of our requirements; but, according to the conditions specified by Him, He will not bring us money, or give it to us, nor help us to obtain it, even though we may be in great need, or in distress. His provision is: "My son, there is plenty for you; the fund is amply sufficient; it is your privilege to draw upon it as freely and as often as you may desire; if you have no faith in my word, if you lack the energy to accept the gifts I offer, then you can receive no help through Me."

The power of God is sufficient to free all mankind from disease and sorrow, misery and failure; but He does not force His healing power, His saving grace, upon any man. He gives man the privilege of drawing to himself all he requires, the stipulation being attached; man must meet the conditions in respect to thought and conduct; he must have sufficient faith to enable him to commence drawing on the account of the Infinite. As faith increases, so will his power take hold of the resources of Infinite Goodness.

These truths the New Commandment inculcates; making it its special object to teach the true doctrine of life to those who are sick and suffering, or in sin and sorrow. Not only do we teach, but we are ready to offer help whenever required. Those who are ready to receive will be given the sublime instructions; we point the way to freedom of body and of soul. Mankind is to be taught what to believe and how to live the Holy (whole) life; resulting in Conscious Individuality, making Health certain.

Chapter Sixteen

God and Nature—the Physicians

Man is of two constituent parts, one as important as the other. His body, the material form, corresponds to the earth, and is under the control of Nature. His Soul, the divine being corresponds to God, and should be under His guidance. When the two (the twain) are in equilibrium, then is man a perfect being.

In stating that the body is ruled over by Nature, and the Soul by God, it is to be understood reference is made to the true man, uncontrolled, guided, or ruled over, by carnal desires.

Contrary to many metaphysical schools, the New Commandment maintains that the flesh is as real and important as the soul or the spirit of man; in fact, we assert that the material is but another expression of spirit, a lower grade of the universal substance, but necessary as a medium through which the soul may express itself; furthermore, that nature is not the enemy of man, but is his guide, "the great physician" to his body, just as God is the Healer to his soul.

The condition termed disease may be of the body or of the mind, or it may be of both body and mind. The true physician, the enlightened teacher, gives careful consideration to both body and soul; he understands that man is ruled either by one or the other, and prescribes his remedies accordingly.

It is not always true that mother Nature, even if given the

opportunity, will be able to heal the sick; for she may be unable to reach the soul of man, though she will always do her best to heal the body. If the soul of man is ill from erroneous and perverted beliefs, thoughts, and desires, Nature alone will be unable to perfect a cure; then the relief for the afflicted soul is effected by God through the instrumentality of man who teaches a wise philosophy, a Wisdom Religion that will bring relief to the troubled Soul.

Fundamentally among the principles of the Christic Interpretation as advocated by the New Commandment, is the doctrine that the material, the physical, the flesh, is real, co-equal with the spirit and the soul of man. The spirit and the soul, can, to a great extent, minister to the material; but, in the main, Nature is the physician. Nature, as a healer, includes all that concerns physical needs; as food, clothing, exercise, work, rest, relaxation, recreation, bathing, breathing, and other normal and natural agencies essential to life. Although the body is substantial and by no means to be underestimated in its importance yet the true man, the divine element, is the soul; that which manifests through the flesh. The flesh, under present physical environments, is the only avenue through which the Immortal part of man can attain its Divine heritage of Conscious unity with God, making Health certain.

There are many ailments of the mind which can be relieved only through the forces of the heart and soul; while there are many diseases of the body induced through a diseased mind and soul. All of these, with the help of Nature, can be eliminated through the effort of the enlightened understanding.

We deny absolutely that the material part of man's being is unreal and without existence, and teach conclusively that it is as truly real in its sphere of action as the spirit and the soul, and essential to these. More than this, it is only through the physical form of man that it becomes possible for God Himself to manifest; therefore, man honors the Creator, *not* by denouncing the flesh, but by *exalting it;* not by denying existence of the body, but by *raising* it to a state of perfection. To glorify God, man must first honor the body, then awaken and illumine the soul. He must make them co-equal through development. In other words, the highest evolvement is reached when man establishes an equilibrium between body and soul the Spirit of God being the central or pivotal point between the two—"and twain have become as one."

The general principles of this philosophy has received attention heretofore; but in consideration of the topic, "God and Nature the physicians," it is fitting to employ a detailed illustration of the methods employed in bringing relief to a sufferer.

For example, let us consider a typical case of the White Plague—Tuberculosis—considered the greatest of all scourges of the present time, but admitted by the world's greatest physicians as due to Mal-nutrition, caused by indulgence in food and drink which congests, so destroying the equilibrium of digestion, assimilation, and elimination.

Consumption is a disease of the body that forms waste, or pus matter, at the expense of healthy tissue; ever feeding upon the healthy tissues to manufacture pus. This formation of pus is accomplished through congestion; herein is both the cause and the basis of relief.

Congestion is always the result of a retardation in the normal process of elimination. The principle of a congested state finds natural illustration in the sewerage system. As long as the sewer is kept open the waste flows freely; but the moment there is interference with the continual flow through the passage, the waste accumulates, congestion results. In the human economy, congestion at any part becomes heated through fermentation; this creates morbid matter which becomes a poison.

Universally man consumes too much food—that is, he ingests a greater amount of food than is required by the system, or that can be successfully eliminated. Thus the body becomes overloaded and all the functions of his organism overtaxed in their effort to throw off the surplus and its effects.

Moreover, few men maintain their organism in such condition as to have the energy to eliminate surplus food material. The result is the same as in the clogged sewer, the unnecessary material is retained in the system; it congests at some point, producing an unnatural heat; the congestion becomes morbid material, and is turned into pus; ever seriously affecting the surrounding tissues.

Various diseases result from this condition. The cause is the same; but, being in different parts of the body, the appelation is according to the location or condition. According to statistics, the most common ailment is Tuberculosis; the reason being found in the fact that surplus food material most naturally settles in the lungs. Why? Because the blood carrying the food particles passes through the lungs, where, according to Nature's Laws, it is to be "burned" and charged with new life, and health-inspiring properties, by the air we breathe. But man, unlike all other animals, does not, as a rule, breathe properly. Being an artificial breather, and not inhaling a sufficient amount of the vivifying and purifying air, he neither sufficiently "burns" up the food carried by the blood so as to be properly prepared for body and tissue building, nor throw out the waste material; consequently, it settles in the lungs and bronchial tubes, and tuberculosis is the natural result.

In the first place, tuberculosis is a disease of the body; brought on either through ignorance of Nature's Laws or deliberate violation of them. Being a physical derangement primarily, it is but natural to draw the inference that Nature alone can affect a cure; that the mind and soul are of little consequence in the treatment of the difficulty.

Such a conclusion, however, is erroneous in the extreme, because consumption is distinctly a negative disease, accompanied by an inert mental attitude. Notwithstanding the fact that the average consumptive believes he will eventually be restored to health and strength, he is disinclined to make the least effort to regain his vital forces. The average victim is particularly affected by a positive unwillingness, even an aversion, to any activity whatsoever that might be conducive to improvement in health. Exercise, so absolutely necessary to stimulate expansive power in the lungs, is decidedly distasteful. In some instances, air , light, and sunshine—Nature's prime restoring agencies—seem to irritate and annoy. Lethargy, indifference, and sluggishness are prominent traits, and stamp the disease as negative in its symptoms. Consequently, in the treatment of this disease, Nature must be supplemented by the mental stimulus.

It is important to arouse and stimulate the patient's mind and soul. He must be convinced that the mental attitude is an indispensable factor in his cure; must be brought to a keen realization that he is created in the image of God, the Father, and can honor and glorify his Maker only by perfecting in himself the Divine Image. He must be thoroughly aroused to the fact that by allowing the image of his Creator to become disease-racked, weakened and miserable, he is dishonoring God, and, in so doing, he is committing as truly a sin as if he were to deliberately violate the most serious moral or legal code. The patient's moral and spiritual sense of responsibility must be thoroughly awakened. He must see and understand that illness is an actual sin, or the result of it; that to disobey a law of health is as grievous as any other form of unrighteousness. As he is responsible for having disregarded the health code, so now it is his duty to restore the equilibrium, and to live in harmony with Nature's laws.

It is essential for every sufferer to understand that violation of Nature's laws in respect to health is a form of unrighteousness; though it may be wise to impress on his mind the positive statements of the principle, and to emphasize the desirability of righteousness rather than the undesirability of error, sin, and weakness. Let him understand that a faithful observance of the laws pertaining to health, strength, and efficiency, is as truly a form of spiritual life as is obedience to the moral decalogue. Especially is it desirable if the sufferer is religiously inclined that he be led to see that righteousness includes observance of hygienic laws, including such homely items as correct habits in regard to diet, sleep, exercise, work, recreation, bathing, and greatest of all, breathing.

In awakening the sufferer's mind to a comprehension of his responsibility, emphasis must be placed on the thought of his privilege, and the desirability and possibility of having health, strength, and vigor. Caution must be exercised to prevent him from settling into a state of mental reflections on the errors of his ways. Cause of illness should be forgotten in the effort of rectifying the error; and the only reason for a patient's knowledge of the first cause of his illness is to enable him to avoid like errors in the future and to remove the cause. He should understand that reversing conditions and removing cause are the only rational means of restoring health, strength, and efficiency. Ambition must be quickened; faith in the possibility of health and strength, intensified; interest in a worthy work or cause, the consciousness of being dear to family, neighbors, and friends; the desire to accomplish a cherished purpose, activities which absorb his attention and interest, and which turn his thoughts from petty symptoms, are all items enabling the mind to cooperate with Nature's healing and restorative agencies and make Health certain.

The principles and arguments of the New Commandment can be employed to good advantage in stimulating mind and soul of the patient to normal activity. He must be convinced that it is not the divine purpose of the Infinite for him to die, but that it is according to the Great Plan for him to live a useful and active life, thereby glorifying his Maker.

At the same time the mind and soul of the sufferer are aroused to activity the physician must give careful consideration to the upbuilding of the physical being; and first in importance is the elimination of congestions from his organism; the decayed food material stored up in his lungs and supplying the fuel for the continuation of the disease. This is accomplished by two methods, both of which are to be followed at the same time. The first is through the medium of daily baths, both external and internal; the second through reducing the allowance of food, giving special attention to the class and quality, and proper combinations.

It is not our desire to outline a dietary regime in this Chapter, as the Humanitarian Society offering detailed instructions to all its members is in a separate text book,* but merely to hint at the importance of the dietary in all cases of illness, no matter what the nature, and especially in Tuberculosis.

A thought in regard to meats. We do not endorse a meat diet; nevertheless, we are not so radical or unreasonable as to expect men, especially the afflicted, to give up meat at once; nor do we consider it wisdom for a person to attempt any sudden, abrupt change in habits of long standing. It is to be noted that Nature's changes are generally slow and gradual; man should learn from her and from his Creator. Taking men as a class, and comprehending that the vast majority are meat eaters, we advocate a gradual change toward the non-meat diet. In the process of this change from one system of life to another, especially in the case of one who is ill, those meats most harmful should be forbidden, while others containing less destructive poisons and acids be substituted, until in time the highly nutritious and easily digested protein foods be entirely substituted for meats.

In effecting the change from weakness and disease to health and strength, it is important the patient be actually anhungered at meal time; then eat only sufficiently to satisfy. This aids digestion and assimilation, reducing the possibility of congestions. Between meals fruits should be served; apples, pine-apples, grape fruits, and other desirable fruits rich in fruit juices and organic mineral elements. Water should be con-

*See the book "Diet, The Way to Health,"

sumed freely and at all times except with meals, though there
are rare exceptions to this rule. Fruit juices, in place of water,
are often highly beneficial and desirable; they not only reduce
a feverish state but supply the valuable building elements to a
debilitated system.

All who are physically impaired, whether from tuberculosis,
nerve exhaustion, or any other chronic ailment, will find it an
excellent plan to eat stewed apples before retiring; these con-
tain every salt required by the system to maintain health. Apples
should not be peeled, but the core may be removed and one or
more tablespoonfuls of honey poured in its place, then baked
until soft and syrup like; eat while still warm, and without the
addition of sugar, milk or cream.

Regulation of diet is only one, though highly important,
means by which nature can effect relief, and it is imperative
the patient shall be active and zealous in promoting such conditions as will enable Nature to perfect her work of healing.
If the sufferer is careless and indifferent in regard to hygienic
requirements, if he obeys instructions with irregularity, indulging his own whims at will, and refuses to actively aid the phy-
sician-teacher, he must expect no more than unsatisfactory progress. Because of this, a disease of negative type demands
firm cooperation of the patient with every natural effort put
forth in his behalf. Heart, mind, spirit, and soul, must co-
operate with Nature and God. It is easy to say that God and
Nature are the only true healers; and as an unqualified statement, it may seem to be a desirable philosophy; yet faith, courage, firmness, patience, and perseverance are required on man's
part, enabling him to create such conditions that God and Na-

ture can perfect their work. Patient as well as physician must work harmoniously, making Health certain.

Equally important with the question of diet is that of breathing; and the patient must be thoroughly aroused to the necessity of continued, conscious, full, deep breathing; and it is well for him to follow exercises which require him to breathe in harmony with Sacred Mantrams or Silent Prayer; thus insuring rythmical as well as deep breathing. Particularly those whose lungs are affected should cultivate habits of correct breathing thereby eliminating poisons from the system; otherwise a state of congestion continues.

Habits in respect to sleeping are also to be corrected; the one suffering to obtain no less than eight hours of sleep in a room well ventilated. The windows should be open night as well as day, in Winter as well as in Summer.

The natural treatment of disease gives attention to exercise as an essential to health and vigor. Outdoor exercise is best; walking is highly recommended; horseback riding is particularly good. Though often it is only by sheer force a patient can be induced to take any kind of wholesome exercise requiring effort, the teacher should persist until obedience is granted; for this reason a philosophy that arouses and stimulates a fondness for activity is of incalculable benefit. The real self, the true being, the Immortal part of the nature, must be quickened to consciousness and activity; this will stimulate an inclination to make effort; will gradually arouse fondness for wholesome exertion; make industry and employment attractive, and counteract the tendency to lethargy and sluggishness which is a noticeable trait in those who suffer, especially in victims of Tuberculosis.

If the patient is faithful to instructions in natural methods of overcoming disease by means of food, drink, sleep, work, exercise, rest, recreation, etc.; if he seeks friendship with light, air, and sunshine; cultivating wholesome habits of thought, eliminating from his mind every type of bitterness and envy; there is no reason why God and Nature should not quickly effect a perfect change in the sufferer; and it is not too much to claim that every case of Tuberculosis, if treated according to these principles, might be cured unless the disease has ravaged the system to a degree where there is no chance of freeing it from congestion and self-poisoning.

Relief of the afflicted according to the natural means here outlined may appear crude to the radical seeker after a negative mysticism or transcendent metaphysics, who foolishly believes the mind to be all-sufficient, and faith alone necessary for the relief of the afflicted. But the rational, well-balanced mind will recognize that natural means combined with reasonable faith in God and Nature and fortified by a sound, constructive Philosophy, is the only true method. Such a system gives due credit to the power of mind and soul; recognizes both God and Nature, both Divine and natural agencies, as well as spirit and matter. It is based on the philosophy that God and Nature are the true regenerators; and points the way by which man may cooperate with them; thus making Health certain.

The Storehouse

"As above, so below," is the Law, and we should reason by comparison. It is as if our earthly parents, having abundant possession, should give us *carte blanche* to draw upon their resources. We have a perfect right to draw upon God's great storehouse to the full extent of our requirements; but, according to the conditions specified by Him, He will not bring us money, or give it to us, nor help us to obtain it, even though we may be in great need, or in distress. His provision is: "My son, there is plenty for you; the fund is amply sufficient; it is your privilege to draw upon it as freely and as often as you may desire; if you have no faith in my word, if you lack the energy to accept the gifts I offer, then you can receive no help through Me."

Chapter Seventeen

God and Nature the Physicians
(Continued)

As previously indicated, Nature includes air, food, drink, exercise and recreation, baths for cleanliness and rejuvenation of body; sunshine, and all other agencies which assist in sustaining the life of the body, and help maintain the health, strength, and vitality of the physical man.

Incredible as it may appear to the thinker, there are many, calling themselves mystics and metaphysicians who, though denying that the physical or material man has real existence, admit that food, air, and drink, are essential to the body (which they claim is a delusion); yet fail to recognize that the quality of food and drink consumed has anything to do with the welfare of the reservoir that receives it. That it is possible for such a belief to find lodging in the minds of men, even of the intellectual classes, is only to be explained on the basis that the race mind has accepted an inconsistent religion or none at all, the average person being unwilling to think, investigate, or analyze for himself anything that pertains to religious matters, laboring under the delusion that he should delegate the subject to priests or ministers just as he depends on the physician for help when ill, rather than educate himself to remain well.

But the time is when man will no longer bow the submissive knee to a philosophy or religion merely because a teacher of prominence promulgates it, demanding one that will bear the test of reason considering them as co-workers, co-creators, life-givers on an equality one with the other. The New Commandment maintains that Nature is the spouse, the hand-maid of God, equally important with Him, because all laws work in Unity, yet only through quality. On the human plane, body and soul holds a similar relationship with one another. In respect to the body, Nature must be consulted and obeyed; while God is the physician to the Soul, often, through the medium of the mind, also to the body. Nature's laws, however, in the healing of mind and body, must be honored and obeyed. In the Christic Interpretation, the New Commandment recognizes there is in reality but one disease; but, like all else in nature, various in its manifestations. This one fundamental ill, this one affliction, may be either of mind or of body; may be caused by wrong thoughts and desires or through incorrect habits of life; ignorance of Nature's laws or a wilful violation of them. In many cases, it may be due to a complication of physical and mental errors.

The multitudes are living in total ignorance of the principles that underlie true foods and a correct combination of them; and countless, otherwise ignorant, farmers are better informed in respect to the treatment of animals and their proper nourishment than they are in regard to the care of themselves or of their families. Many men are making a careful study of the conditions that help to develop livestock to the highest point of beauty and utility; whereas, respecting mankind, they are content to live in accordance with the custom and habits of their ancestors, regardless of the wisdom or advisability of so doing.

The blood coursing through the veins of man is his life; but the life-fluid can be healthful and vitalizing only as it is made thus through partaking of the right class of food. It is impossible to have pure blood unless proper nourishment is supplied. Purity of thought and desire, no matter how holy and lofty they may be, in themselves cannot insure purity of blood; this the New Commandment teaches as a fundamental law; and mental and physical conditions must supplement each other; mind alone is not all powerful; thought alone cannot effect perfect physical states; therefore, we maintain that food, pure in quality and harmonious in combination, is essential not alone to health, but is *absolutely necessary if there is to be spiritual elevation and moral strength.*

Moreover, in its instructions regarding the correct habits of life, the New Commandment teaches there is a proper, as well as an improper, time for eating. In general, the correct time is indicated by Nature's call—actual hunger. To eat when one is not anhungered is nothing less than storing disease in one's system. Nature has so constituted man and his organism that there will be no release of the digestive fluids in the stomach and intestines unless he is actually hungry. Consequently, without this demand for food the system is not in condition to make digestion and assimilation possible.

Food taken into the stomach when it is not ready to receive it, greatly delays digestion; fermentation frequently commences and the contents of the stomach may even reach a stage of putrefaction. When, finally, the food is changed into fluid and assimilated, instead of being normal and full of life-giving power, it is actually poisonous to the system; and only the resisting power of the body prevents man from quickly succumbing to these toxins. It may be years before the body is finally destroyed through their effects; or there may be much suffering from various so-called diseases. It is now universally recognized that

many cases of insanity, as well as much crime, is directly due
to Toxo-absorption (usually termed auto-intoxication); this is
in reality a poisoning of the system through indiscreet habits of
eating, non-digestion of food, and imperfect elimination. Primarily this was due to an excess of food, improper combinations,
inferior quality, or to such as are not adapted to the consumer's
requirements. Under these conditions the material is neither
fully digested nor assimilated, nor is there full elimination; this
results in the manufacture of toxins, which, entering the blood
stream, induce acidosis, or poisoning.

Correct habits in respect to diet, though extremely important in both physical, *mental, and moral* health, is only one of
Nature's means of maintaining health and strength; another is
the art of breathing. None can be healthy and strong who do
not breathe freely and deeply of pure, fresh air. It is unquestionably true that men have been able to live many years who
did not breath properly; and even such as lived mostly indoors
attained old age; but it is impossible to determine how much
longer they might have lived had they been subject to normal
conditions. If man were to breathe deeply and properly of
fresh air at all times, it would be possible for him to partake
of inferior food, even such as are now a poison to him; because
when the food essences passed through the lungs, the deep breath
ing of pure air would extract the poisonous material from them
and throw them out of the system. Nevertheless, even though
this be possible, it is by no means advisable to tax the lungs
with unnecessary work. It is, however, a fact well worth knowing; for most of us are at times so situated that we cannot avail
ourselves of correct food. Under temporary conditions of this
nature, we need not fear harmful results if we consciously co-

operate with the lungs in freeing the system of deleterious sub-. stances. However, since man is ordinarily an artificial breather, elimination of poisons is not accomplished to any great extent by the lungs; poisonous substances, therefore, must be eliminated in some other manner, as, through the pores of the skin, the kidneys, or the bowels; otherwise they remain in the system, disturbing mind and body, inducing physical and spiritual disability.

As pure food and air are essential to all men in the flesh whether they are the highest mystics or the humblest artisans, so, also, is sunshine. It is through the rays of the sun that man receives vitality, a magnetic force that makes for life and power just as the suns rays shining on the earth enables it to produce abundantly the plants and the herbs required by all living creatures. Were it not for the rays of the sun striking the earth and having magnetic intercourse with it, charging it with life-power, there would either be no vegetation or it would be a poisonous fungus. It is a noteworthy fact that deadly weeds grow under trees and brushes and in dense forests where the rays of the sun do not penetrate. That sunshine is essential to physical welfare is recognized by practically every Sanitarium; sun parlors affording the patient opportunity for basking in the suns rays and becoming charged with new life and vigor.

Sleep is another of Nature's means of promoting health and vigor. For centuries it has been accepted as a truth that the strength of man is derived from the food he consumed; this is no longer regarded as a fact. Men have overlooked the importance of sleep in its relation to strength and vitality. Food, like fire in the engine, produces heat and motive power; but the energy is secured from the water in the engine which becomes heated through the consuming of fuel, and generates steam.

Likewise, the food consumed, by creating the necessary heat, is merely the means of furnishing the power. During sleep, when assimilation is taking place, and pure air is inbreathed, the body receives the strength and the energy that gives life and vigor; a sufficient number of hours of sleep is essential to health, strength, and vitality, irrespective of man's station in life, whether living a purely animal existence, or the most exalted spiritual life.

Nevertheless, even perfect relaxation and wholesome sleep are dependent upon other conditions, particularly dietary discretion and an abundance of pure fresh air. There can be no health —inducing sleep if digestion is abnormal. When there is assimilation of toxins instead of life-giving, energizing substances, sleep is disturbed. If there is a lack of fresh air in the sleeping chamber, natural combustion is interfered with; as in the stove having no draft the fire is liable to die out. There should always be an abundant circulation of fresh air in the human organism (lungs) insuring the fires that aid in changing the food into a vital force, thus making Health certain.

Dietary indiscretion is not the only cause of illness, nor is the correction of the dietary the only means of regaining health and efficiency. Wisdom in the selection and preparation of food, an abundant supply of fresh air, wholesome exercise and activity, frequent access to the genial rays of the sun, plenty of pure liquids, elevating occupation,—all are essential to physical and mental health and efficient work; neither one or the other alone is sufficient; but a rational, harmonious combination of them all, will work wonders in establishing health, power, and strength. Combining these measures with wholesome, constructive, optimistic thought-habits and a masterful will we have a rational system of life. All these should be observed by the natural man; nor is it at all difficult so to do, though it may seem otherwise to those who have merely existed, lo, these many years.

It is hardly possible to lay too much stress on the import- ance of dietary observation. Practically the whole life depends on the food one consumes. More ills of life are due to this one item than mankind has thought possible. An excess of stim- ulating food creates a desire for alcoholic drink; or, it may arouse to an abnormal degree the carnal nature, and intensify tendencies toward crime and lust. In either case, the evil is en- tirely dependent for its existence on the heat generated in the body by the improper food. The heat thus generated is not nor- mal; it is an irritation; it is an incentive toward unnatural acts, and to it we may trace the twin evils,—drunkenness and traffic in white slavery. As long as men continue to inflame stomach, blood, and brain with irritating food, just that long will crime exist, nor will it be overcome until man learns to live a rational life.

When men and women eat according to reason and dietary law, and observe other natural decrees, there will no longer be generated abnormal heat, nor irritation of the nerves to be com- municated to the brain. The demands of the body, however, will not be destroyed, weakened or impaired; rather, as a re- sult of discretion, they will become natural and trustworthy and require merely normal, reasonable satisfaction.

The New Commandment does not deal merely with results; but aims, instead, to correct the trouble at its root. Social evils, like cancer, may be apparently removed while in reality the cause of the difficulty remains in the social organism. So long as there is one root remaining in the social body, it is certain again to grow; and, as with cancer, every new growth will be more virulent than the former.

The New Commandment maintains that neither the evils of alcohol nor those of prostitution can be removed through legislative enactments; nor can desire be controlled by legal decrees or legislative power in the hands of associated physicians, no matter how extensive their learning. Such evils, in fact, all that is degrading, can be removed only by fortifying mankind with knowledge and *removing the cause;* this is two-fold—primary and secondary; and reveals itself in the mode of a man's life, in his manner of eating, sleeping, breathing, exercising, and labor. *Moreover, all these determine, to an unthought extent, the character of his thoughts and desires.*

It is easy to declare that evil originates in man's thoughts, that the beginning of sin is in "the imaginations of the thoughts of the heart." But a rational adjustment of all things demands recognition of the fact that soundness of body is essential to purity of mind; that it is well-nigh, if not altogether impossible, for an individual to be actuated by lofty aspirations and hopeful views pertaining to life, when his physical being is disturbed by poisonous accretions or famished for vitalizing food elements. It is necessary to remove the secondary cause as well as the primary; removing the secondary, and making physical conditions as nearly perfect as possible, will help in the removal of the primary. The mental and physical must work together, that mind and body are supplementary agencies in establishing health and efficiency, that God and Nature are inseparable—this the New Commandment maintains as a fundamental truth; and on it as a foundation must it stand or fall.

Is there basis for this doctrine in revealed religion—in the Sacred Scriptures?

There is. Listen to these words, coming down to us through the ages in thundering tones:

"What satisfieth thy mouth with good things, so that thy youth is renewed like the eagles."

How many of the vast multitudes who have read these words ever gave a thought to their meaning?

Yet how significant! How thoroughly in harmony with the doctrine of Life and Immortality; the New Commandment, that "filling the mouth with good things" is a requisite of the Immortality whose "youth is renewed like the eagles!"

Let us hope this important passage in the Scripture may be more than a dead letter to all who read it in the light of the Christic Interpretation; that humankind may hasten to accept the truth in its simplicity. Let no mystic or metaphysician regard it a materialistic doctrine which advocates that the youth of him whose mouth the Lord filleth with good things—natural, nutritious food—is renewed like the eagles.

"Bless the Lord, O my soul; and all that is within me, bless his holy (whole) name.

"Bless the Lord, O my soul, and forget not all his benefits.

"Who forgiveth all thine iniquities; who healeth all thy disease;

"Who redeemeth thy life from destruction; who crowneth thee with loving kindness and tender mercies;

"Who satisfieth thy mouth with good things, so that thy youth is renewed like the eagles."—Ps. 103:1-5.

These verses, in exalted poetic expression, voice the doctrine of Life and Immortality. They honor God as the Giver of all good things; and man as the recipient of them, or as the medium through whom the Infinite functions. These words portray a well-balanced philosophy; one that represents God and man as counterparts; each of the other; God and Nature as harmonious co-workers; a philosophy that recognizes physical means and agencies as thoroughly consistent with spiritual laws and divine graces.

If the soul is to be pure and exalted, cleanse the body first; this is the way to Conscious Individuality; is making Heatlh certain.

CPSIA information can be obtained at www.ICGtesting.com
Printed in the USA
LVOW10s0245100316

478465LV00024B/846/P